Tear Catchers

Developing the Gift of Compassion

Tear Catchers

Developing the Gift of Compassion

HAROLD IVAN SMITH [pseud.

[JASON TOWNER)

ABINGDON PRESS

Nashville

TEAR-CATCHERS

Copyright © 1984 by Abingdon Press

Library of Congress Cataloging in Publication Data

Tear-catchers.
Includes bibliographical references.
1. Sympathy—Religious aspects—Christianity.
I. Title.
BV4647.S9T68   1984   248.4   84-9221

ISBN 0-687-41184-X

Scripture quotations unless otherwise noted are taken from
The Holy Bible: New International Version. Copyright ©
1978 by the New York International Bible Society. Used by
permission of Zondervan Bible Publishers.

MANUFACTURED BY THE PARTHENON PRESS AT
NASHVILLE, TENNESSEE, UNITED STATES OF AMERICA

*This book is dedicated to two
practitioners of tear-catching*

John A. Larsen, Ph.D.
J. Michael Smith, M.D.

*two tear-catchers who are
making a difference
in our world*

ACKNOWLEDGMENTS

In the intersections of our lives we meet individuals who dare to share ideas, explain concepts, listen to hunches, and occasionally smile and nod.

I am grateful to a host of individuals who have contributed to the development of the concept of tear-catching: James L. Garlow, Hugh Eichelburger, Reuben Welch, David Haas, Bruce Larson, Ron Attrell, Joe Ford, Bette Neale, Betty Benjesdorf, Mary Randolph, Sandi Watson, Sharon Matthews, and Frank Freed.

CONTENTS

It is good for us to think no grace or blessing truly ours till we are aware that God has blessed someone else with it through us.

Not by mere moods, not by how I feel to-day or how I felt yesterday may I know whether I am indeed living the life of God, but by knowing that God is using me to help others.

Phillips Brooks
The Light of the World
London: Macmillan, 1899

INTRODUCTION

Nashville, Tennessee, my home for nine years, is best known as the home of country music—the Nashville Sound. Country music has made the tear-jerker into an art form. Tear-jerkers are songs that talk about "somebody done somebody wrong."

A lot of people—not just country music singers—know how to jerk tears. But who catches the tears after they fall?

That question became the idea for this book. It began in a little restaurant in Kansas City as a group of men ate lunch. In the course of the conversation one man announced he wanted someone to write his biography. "I need someone like Smith here who really knows how to jerk the tears," he told us. He was referring to *Jason Loves Jane*, which has been called by some a handkerchief book—you need a few when you read the book.

It was then the idea struck me: what our society needs is tear-*catchers*. What is a tear-catcher?

A tear-catcher is a person who catches someone else's tears without intimidating the person or interfering with the process. As I help another person, my yesterday becomes someone's tomorrow, because I am sharing what

I have learned. My tears can become an oasis for the next weary pilgrim on the trail.

A father was concerned because his daughter was late coming home from a neighbor's house where she had gone to play. When she finally arrived, he sternly demanded, "Why are you late?"

"Becky dropped her doll and broke it," she reported. The father mentally raced ahead and responded, "And I suppose you were helping her pick up the pieces?"

"No," she said. "I was helping her cry."

Somewhere a man, a woman, a child weeps alone. All of us have experienced that moment. I have. There were those who could have caught my tears, who could have helped me cry, but they did not. As a result I am tempted to focus on my lack of self-control; that is, if I had been more of a man I wouldn't have been crying in the first place; I would not have embarrassed others.

> Well, I have come to a conclusion.
>> It is those who are resistant to tears
>>> who most need
>>> to release them.
>> Whatever a tear weighs
>>> it is never as heavy
>>> as the burden which created it.

Being a tear-catcher is a bit like helping someone move. While you're trying to get a big piece of furniture up the stairs or through the door, there comes the moment when someone says, "Hold up a minute." While that person tries to get a better grip, the other movers have to shoulder or bear most of the weight.

I am a struggler. I still have to say, "Hold up a minute. Help me."

I'm still on the journey. I haven't "arrived" in any sense of the word. There are days I stand staring at the road map trying to comprehend the directions. I need all the help I can get.

You may say at this point, "Hey, wait a minute. I paid good money for this book and you're telling me that you are still struggling and don't have all the answers?"

That's right. I don't. I'm still learning. And I need you to catch some of my tears. I can't catch my own very well; I get blinded and somehow they escape my hand. At the same time, I'll try to catch some of yours. Because tear-catching is God's work.

After the birth of Isaac, Sarah demanded that Abraham send the servant girl Hagar and her son Ishmael away into the desert. The request distressed Abraham "greatly because it concerned his son" (Gen. 21:11). Yet Abraham obeyed God's directions and sent them out "with some food and a skin of water" (verse 14). In those days travelers were given only enough provisions to make it to the next settlement or village. Somehow, Hagar got lost.

Inevitably the water and food ran out and death began stalking their trail. Finally, Hagar put the boy under some bushes and wandered a short distance from him. There she broke down and wept. "I cannot watch the boy die," she screamed (verse 16).

But "God heard the boy crying and the angel of God called to Hagar from heaven and said to her, '. . . Do not be afraid. . . . Lift the boy up and take him by the hand, for I will make him into a great nation' " (verses 17-18).

"Then God opened her eyes and she saw a well" (verse 19). Perhaps the well had been there all along and she had been blinded by her tears. On the other hand, the tears may have cleansed her eyes so that she could see God's faithfulness.

God, the Great Being, the Creator, heard a boy's cries in the wilderness. That tells us he can hear us cry.

There are legions of people today crying in wildernesses of their own or another's making. Will they be abandoned in those deserts? Or can we go to them, become tear-catchers, open their eyes to the wells of help available for their need?

I hope you'll begin the journey.

1
TEARS: A BIBLICAL PERSPECTIVE

Every man, every woman is born to cry. Crying is usually our first act outside the womb. That first whack from an obstetrician or midwife shocks us from the peace of the womb into the harsh reality called life. How many mothers, after long-troubled childbirth, have then wept in concert with the child?

In the days of home births, the baby's cry broke the strain of tense waiting. The congratulations began. Then the family waited for the doctor's or midwife's news: boy or girl, healthy or unhealthy.

How appropriate that we should be endowed by the Creator with the gift of tears! The writer of Ecclesiastes observed:

There is a time for everything
and a season for every activity under heaven:
a time to be born and a time to die,
. . .
a time to weep and a time to laugh. (3:1, 4)

Ah, but we prefer to laugh. Indeed, we have hordes of professional laugh-producers or comedians to make us laugh. Yet someone has noted that behind every great laugh-giver is one who equally knows how to cry.

In fact, the two processes were not just coincidentally linked by the writer of Ecclesiastes. "He laughed until he cried" is a common saying, as is "I didn't know whether to laugh or to cry." As a funeral director, I often observed that phenomenon: one moment a parlor where a family received visitors was hushed and quiet; the next moment, polite, yet relief-giving laughter echoed.

Every person cries from the fourth month on. The intricate design of the tear process works like an automatic pilot to keep the crying apparatus continually primed, available for implementation on a moment's notice.

When we realize we are designed to cry, when we stand in the mind's eye with the great biblical examples, we feel no shame.

Can you picture Joseph weeping at the reunion with his cruel brothers who had sold him into slavery?

Can you stand in the dark shadows of Gethsemane, eavesdropping as Jesus wept?

Can you see the impatient Peter squirming as he is surrounded by weeping women mourning Dorcas' death?

Can you hear the wrenching sobs from him after the cock crowed the third time?

Perhaps it is because I have a vivid imagination that I let my mind's eye create that room in Pharaoh's palace to which Joseph fled; that cell in a damp prison where Paul wept for the young churches; King David's couch in his Jerusalem home.

Tears have punctuated the Bible. Can you grieve with Esau as he protested Jacob's trickery? Can you feel Eve's wet tears as she learned of Abel's death? Can you sense Esther's tears for her people?

In a close reading, the Bible becomes a mirror. We feel a oneness with the heroes of the faith: they too cried. But we also sense the fear of tears, that firmly entrenched cultural bias against them. Why else would Joseph have fled? Somewhere, at some dark moment in human history, someone—some group—decided that tears were inappropriate; others said "only under certain conditions." Thus tears became restricted, less treasured.

That sin—that denial of the God-givenness of tears—has been visited not only on the third and fourth generations, but has been passed from father-to-son-to-son-to-son. That's why today we must have paid laughter-causers or comedians. We seek laughter as a cosmetic to cover up the true range of our emotions.

If we felt freer to cry—if we felt less a need to distract one another from our tears—we would be healthier.

The Word of God allows me to hear the tears of God's saints. So awe-struck am I by their tears that I realize I need feel no shame in shedding mine.

Let's examine some biblical models. The first recorded biblical weeper is Abraham, a man of rich emotions and "God's friend" (James 2:23). It should be noted here, though, that laughter appears first in Scripture. Abraham laughed when God revealed that Sarah would give birth to a child (Gen. 17:17).

THE FIRST TEARS WERE PRODUCED
BY MOURNING

When Sarah died at the ripe old age of 127, Abraham went to Kiriath Arba "to mourn for Sarah and to weep over her" (Gen. 23:2). Our colloquial term "weep over" or "about" someone or something may have originated because people stood over the body of a loved one and spilled their tears.

Jacob wept for Joseph after he was presented with Joseph's coat of many colors, which had been dipped in goat's blood (Gen. 37:35) and "he refused to be comforted." Years later, upon their reunion in Goshen,

Joseph "threw his arms around his father, and wept for a long time" (Gen. 46:29). Later, when Jacob died, "Joseph threw himself upon his father and wept over him and kissed him" (Gen. 50:1). We feel no embarrassment over his masculine display of emotions.

In a later instance, David marched in Abner's funeral procession "and wept aloud at Abner's tomb." David's example was followed by the people (II Sam. 3:32). When David sang Abner's funeral lament, "all the people wept over him again" (3:34). But David also cried as he "pleaded with God" for the life of the child born to Bathsheba (II Sam. 12:16, 21). He "and all his servants" wept "very bitterly" when news reached him of the murder of his son Amnon (13:36) by Absalom. At another time he wept over Absalom.

> The king was shaken. He went up to the room over the gateway and wept. As he went, he said "O my son Absalom! My son, my son Absalom! If only I had died instead of you—O Absalom, my son, my son!" (II Sam. 18:33)

Yet David failed to comfort his weeping daughter Tamar after she was raped by Amnon (II Sam. 13). In fact, Absalom told her, "Be quiet now, my sister; he is your brother. Don't take this thing to heart" (13:20).

Another man of God, Ezekiel, was commanded *not* to cry at the death of his wife.

> The word of the Lord came to me: "Son of man, with one blow I am about to take away from you the delight of your eyes. Yet *do not lament or weep or shed any tears.* Groan quietly; do not mourn for the dead. . . ."
>
> So I spoke to the people in the morning, and in the evening my wife died. The next morning I did as I had been commanded. (Ezek. 24:15-18, italics mine)

This became a powerful witness to the Jews of what was to come.

In the New Testament period, crying at death was still customary, as were professional mourners. In reporting Lazarus' death, John noted, "When Jesus saw her weeping, and the Jews who had come along with her also weeping, he was deeply moved" (John 11:33). This is a prelude to the oft-quoted yet oft-misunderstood thirty-fifth verse, "Jesus wept." A careful reading of the text shows that Jesus wept *before* he saw the tomb. He was crying at the people's failure to understand his mission. The thirty-eighth verse reports, "Jesus, *once more deeply moved*, came to the tomb" (italics mine).

The mourning illustrated hopelessness that only the Resurrection could end. In Luke's Gospel, the physician reports the death of the only son of a widow (a striking parallel to Jesus' death). "When the Lord saw her, his heart went out to her and he said, 'Don't cry' " (Luke 7:13). That seems particularly uncompassionate—unless we understand that Jesus was suggesting her tears were premature. Verse fifteen observes, "Jesus gave him [the deceased] back to his mother."

The third encounter of Jesus with hysteria is reported by Mark. When Jesus traveled to the home of the synagogue ruler whose daughter had died, he "saw a commotion, with people crying and wailing loudly" (Mark 5:38). So he asked what was going on. ("Why all this commotion and wailing?") When Jesus reported the little girl was only asleep, the crowds laughed (verses 39-40).

So Jesus promptly "put them all out" (verse 40) and, in the presence of the parents and the disciples, brought her back to life. There must have been the slightest trace of a smile as he left town hearing the Jews arguing among themselves, "But I tell you she *was* dead!"

John noted that in heaven the cause of crying will be eliminated. "There will be no more death or mourning or crying"; these are all part of "the old order of things [that] has passed away" (Rev. 21:4).

TEARS WERE AN INDEX OF EMOTIONS

Tamar, after being raped by her own brother, wept "aloud as she went" to her brother's home (II Sam. 13:19). That hideous act produced the civil strife that cost David two sons, Amnon and Absalom. Yet she received no comfort from her protective brother or from her father, although the latter was reportedly "furious" (verse 21). It is incongruous that David wept so freely and sang so commonly of tears—yet failed to be a tear-catcher to his own daughter; such may be more an indictment of the cultural low value placed on women than a commentary on David's compassion.

Jephthah's daughter inherited the emotional pain when she fully realized the implications of her father's decision to sacrifice "whatever comes out of the door of my house to meet me when I return in triumph from the Ammonites" (Judg. 11:31). Before he could comply, she made only one request: "Give me two months to roam the hills and weep with my friends because I will never marry" (11:37). So her friends became the first collective tear-catchers and helped her put the emotional shock into perspective.

When David and Jonathan realized that both could not survive Saul's madness, they met in a field and "wept together" (I Sam. 20:41). The grief had to be enormous, the anticipation of death menacing, because Jonathan loved David "as he loved himself" (20:17). Yet, in this meeting, Samuel reported that "David wept the most" (20:41), which may have been indicative of the depth of his sorrow.

Another glimpse is seen in the unique relationship of the two tear-catchers. On the surface, Jonathan had the most to gain if Saul succeeded in killing David. Yet, as David wandered the desert hills of Ziph, "Saul's son Jonathan went to David at Horesh and helped him find strength in God" (I Sam. 23:16).

PEOPLE CRIED FROM FEAR

Saul wept when he realized how easily David could have killed him in a cave near the Craig of the Wild Goats (I Sam. 24:16). David, however, was conscience-stricken because he had threatened God's anointed king.

Shortly thereafter, when the Amalekites raided Ziklag and took the women captive, "David and his men wept aloud until they had no strength left to weep" (I Sam. 30:4). Although David's tears were motivated by the capture of his two wives (Ahinoam and Abigail), they were also influenced by the awareness that his men "were talking of stoning him" (30:6*a*).

PEOPLE CRIED FOR JOY

When Jacob saw Rachel the first time, he kissed her and "began to weep aloud" (Gen. 29:11).

As the foundation for the Temple was laid, "Many of the older priests and Levites and family heads, who had seen the former temple, wept aloud"; others "shouted for joy" (Ezra 3:12). This mixture of emotions produced some confusion. "No one could distinguish the sound of the shouts of joy from the sound of weeping, because the people made so much noise. And the sound was heard far away" (verse 13).

PEOPLE CRIED FROM BROKEN HEARTS

When the Jews were carried of into Babylonian captivity they "sat and wept" when they remembered Zion. In fact, they hung their harps on the poplar trees when their captors jested, "Sing us one of the songs of Zion," to which the Jews retorted, "How can we sing the songs of the Lord while in a foreign land?" (Ps. 137:1, 3, 4).

The Psalms give us a unique insight into crying.

I am worn out from groaning;
  all night long I flood my bed with weeping
  and drench my couch with tears. (Ps. 6:6)

My tears have been my food day and night. (Ps. 42:3)

You have fed them with the bread of tears;
  you have made them drink tears by the bowlful. (Ps. 80:5)

For I eat ashes as my food
  and mingle my drink with tears. (Ps. 102:9)

Many who weep today, after nights of tear-stained pillow cases and days of not eating, can identify with David.

Jeremiah prophesied of brokenness, that those who returned to Jerusalem would "come with weeping" (Jer. 31:9). But he also prophesied of the distress of the last days;

A voice is heard in Ramah,
  mourning and great weeping
Rachel weeping for her children
  and refusing to be comforted. (Jer. 31:15, italics mine)

PEOPLE CRIED IN HELPLESSNESS

Sometimes there seems to be nothing we can do but cry. How many times have parents responded, "Well, crying's not going to make it any better"? But that is not altogether true. In the Old Testament a faithful man named Elkanah had two wives, one with children, the other barren. Hannah, the barren wife, faithfully prayed for a child. But "her rival provoked her till she wept and would not eat" (I Sam. 1:7). Giving us a rare glimpse of a tender man, the writer emphasized that Elkanah was concerned. "Hannah, why are you weeping? Why don't you eat? Why are you downhearted? Don't I mean more to you than ten sons?" (verse 8).

Yet Hannah wanted a son. Finally, "in bitterness of soul Hannah wept much and prayed to the Lord," (verse 10), vowing that if she could become pregnant she would give the child to the Lord.

The prophet Eli saw her praying in the court of the worship tent and thought she was drunk. But she retorted, "I am a woman who is deeply troubled. . . . I was pouring out my soul to the Lord" (verse 15). Eventually she conceived and gave birth to Eli's successor, Samuel.

When David became king, he demanded that his first wife Michal be returned (in anger Saul had given her to Paltiel). Ish-Bosheth "had her taken away from her husband." But Paltiel "went with her, weeping behind her all the way to Bahurim" (II Sam. 3:15, 16).

Either Paltiel was an idiot to have been so unmanly as to cry in front of the king's men or he deeply loved her. Yet he was helpless against the king's wishes.

Finally Abner said, "Go back home!" (verse 16). And Paltiel did just that. Sometimes we conclude nothing can be done and we must live with that reality. Paltiel could not go on weeping forever.

Another illustration of helplessness is seen in Esau's response after his father had mistakenly blessed Jacob, as a result of their mother's scheme. "He burst out with a loud and bitter cry and said to his father, 'Bless me—me too, my father!' " (Gen. 27:34). He repeated the request, "Do you have only one blessing, my father?" (verse 38). "Then Easu wept aloud" in response to the irreversibility of the blessing. The writer of Hebrews later noted, "He could bring about no change of mind, though he sought the blessing with tears" (Heb. 12:17).

In the New Testament, we sense Peter's helplessness as the rooster crowed. Matthew reported that "he wept bitterly" (Matt. 26:75), while Mark noted that "he broke down and wept" (Mark 14:72). He wept because he had failed the only one who could help him.

Another insight into helplessness occurs somewhat ironically in the Revelation. John wept when he realized that "no one in heaven or on earth or under the earth could open the scroll. . . . *I wept and wept*" until "one of the elders said to me, 'Do not weep! See, the Lion of the Tribe of Judah, the Root of David, has triumphed' " (Rev. 5:3-5, italics mine).

PEOPLE WEPT FOR THEIR COMMITMENTS

Esther fell at King Xerxes' feet (risking her life by approaching him without an invitation) and through her tears pleaded for his intervention to stop Haman's plot to execute the Jews.

When Nehemiah heard of the broken walls of Jerusalem, he "sat down and wept" (Neh. 1:4).

Ezra wept over his people's marriage to foreign women (Ezra 10:1).

Tears are best illustrated by Jeremiah, "the weeping prophet."

> Oh, that my head were a spring of waters
>   and my eyes a fountain of tears!
> I would weep day and night
>   for the slain of my people. (Jer. 9:1)

However, the people were not always sympathetic. "Let's attack him with our tongues and pay no attention to anything he says" (Jer. 18:18). Eventually the prophet's ideas got him thrown into a muddy cistern of Malkijah.

In the New Testament, we glimpse the tears of Jesus as he struggled to understand God's design. Hebrews reports, "He offered up prayers and petitions with loud cries and tears" (5:7).

Paul's writing and preaching were marked by tears. In his farewell to the Ephesian elders he remarked, "I served the Lord with great humility and with tears" (Acts 20:19). He called attention to his faithfulness. "Remember that for three years I never stopped warning each of you night and day with tears" (Acts 20:31). And who could forget the pathos of those final moments of Paul with the elders? "They all wept as they embraced him and kissed him. What grieved them most was his statement that they would never see his face again" (Acts 20:37-38).

But Paul had to be firm in his commitment; he could not be swayed by the tears of those who loved him. At Caesarea the people pleaded with him not to go to Jerusalem. Paul responded, "Why are you weeping and breaking my heart? I am ready not only to be bound, but also to die in Jerusalem for the name of the Lord Jesus" (Acts 21:13). Apparently the dialogue continued, for Luke reported, "When he would not be dissuaded, we gave up and said, 'The Lord's will be done' " (verse 14).

Paul's letter to the Philippians reported, "For, as I have often told you before and now say again even with tears, many live as enemies of the cross of Christ" (Phil. 3:18).

OBSERVATIONS

With such a rich heritage and tradition of tears, none of us—men or women—should feel ashamed to cry today. Yet somewhere in history someone decided that men should not cry. As a Jew, Joseph should have felt no shame in crying. Yet, when reunited with his brothers, he "hurried out and looked for a place to weep" (Gen. 43:30). Perhaps this was to protect his identity from his brothers or to protect his image from the Egyptians.

In a tradition apparently as old as mankind, men have learned to control their tears. "Then Joseph could no longer control himself before all his attendants" (Gen. 45:1), so he ordered everyone out. However, "he wept so loudly that the Egyptians heard him, and Pharoah's household heard about it" (verse 2).

Tears were part of the fabric of family, friendship, and worship. Much of the sacred writing reports that events, edicts, and king's orders were overruled by tears. The tears of the baby Moses softened the heart of Pharaoh's daughter (Exod. 2:5-7) to the point that she dared ignore her father's proclamation.

Observation 1: Tears Evoke a Wide Range of Reactions

Little children are fascinated by tears and crying. A child who sees someone crying asks, "Why is he crying?" It must be particularly confusing when an adult cries. In fact, many of us play a game with children in which we pretend to cry so we can watch the child's swift change of reaction. This must be particularly confusing for a child who has been repeatedly told, "Only sissies cry."

Tears cannot be ignored; they always produce a response: surprise? contempt? empathy?

Isaiah prophesied, "Look, their brave men cry aloud in the streets; the envoys of peace weep bitterly" (Isa. 33:7). John prophesied that in the awful day, "the merchants of the earth will weep" (Rev. 18:11). The response can be as significant as the tear.

Observation 2: Tears, Then and Now, Must Be Explained!

Tears must be explained. The first moments of developing an authentic tear-catcher are when a parent explains someone's tears to a child. If the tears of another child or an adult are too easily dismissed, the child will question his or her own tears as well as the value of tears in general.

Initially, children note the social context of the tear: the surroundings. They even make judgments. Eventually they ask for explanations. Thus children come to find rationales that may support their own tears. In essence, they reason that if other children can cry, so can I!

The Bible reports that tears have often been questioned. When the Lord revealed to Elisha the fate of the Israelites under Hazael, the prophet wept. That provoked the king's question, "Why is my lord weeping?" (II Kings 8:12).

When Nahash the Ammonite offered a treaty only by gouging out one eye of every Jew, the emotional impact humiliated the people. Saul, upon returning from the fields (unaware of the demands), asked, "What is wrong with the people? Why are they weeping?" (I Sam. 11:5).

The angels asked Mary at the tomb, "Woman, why are you crying?" (John 20:13), and Jesus repeated the same question. Apparently Mary did not recognize his voice, for she assumed he was the gardener.

Observation 3: Leadership Is Significant

In the 1972 New Hampshire primary, there seemed to be a ground swell for a politician named Edmund Muskie. He was a neighbor from Maine, and yet his campaign fizzled.

A newspaper attacked the character of his wife, and Muskie called a press conference. He wept in defending her honor.

The press then asked, "Can we have a man as president who cannot control his emotions?"

Yet the Bible documents that all the great men (as well as many of the failures) have cried. Indeed, what makes a man cry may be the most accurate photograph of his soul. And when a leader feels comfortable enough with his emotions to cry, so will others.

Observation 4: The Lord Responds to Tears

To say that the Lord responds to tears is not to say that he can be manipulated by tears. LaVerne Tripp's hit song puts it accurately: "Tears Are a Language God Understands."

Somehow we have developed the notion of a God who cannot cry. If that assumption were true and we wanted to follow his example, it would be noble that we not cry. However, I suggest that a false understanding of God has further frustrated us—men particularly—and blocked us from a healthy psychological and spiritual release through crying.

If God the Son cried while on earth, why should I feel any less a man or a child of God if I cry? Hebrews 5:7 makes it clear that God heard the "loud cries and tears" of Jesus. As the supreme leader, Jesus felt no risk in crying before his disciples. If he could cry, cannot I?

Our assumption of a tearless God is based upon our reading of Revelation 21:4b, "There will be no more death or mourning or crying or pain, for the old order of things has passed away." A popular gospel classic declared, "No tears in heaven," while another one insisted, "Teardrops will never stain the streets of that city."

However, we overlook 4a: "He will wipe every tear from their eyes." So all pilgrims will have to initially have tears in heaven. How could God have been tearless on that first Good Friday as he heard his son plead, "My God, my God, why have you forsaken me?" (Matt. 27:46)?

A tearless God could not have ignored the mothers' tears and wailing in a blood-soaked Bethlehem after Herod's rage.

He is the God who sees our tears. The Lord instructed Isaiah to tell Hezekiah, "I have heard your prayer and seen your tears" (Isa. 38:5), and then added fifteen years to the life of the king.

David, who was no stranger to tears, wrote, "The Lord has heard my weeping" (Ps. 6:8) and "delivered . . . my eyes from tears" (Ps. 116:8).

Thus we witness the promise of a responsive God. "O people of Zion, . . . you will weep no more. How gracious he will be when you cry for help! As soon as he hears, he will answer you" (Isa. 30:19).

But his ease with tears was best demonstrated by his Son. When Jesus dined at a certain Pharisee's house, a woman "who had lived a sinful life" brought an alabaster jar of perfume. "As she stood behind him at his feet weeping, she began to wet his feet with her tears. Then she wiped them with her hair, kissed them and poured perfume on them."

But observe Jesus' poise; he is not shaken by the experience as is the Pharisee who says, "If this man were a prophet, he would know who is touching him and what kind of woman she is—that she is a sinner" (Luke 7:37-39). All that is missing is an exclamation mark to summarize his attitude.

In an act of graciousness, Jesus is able to accept a woman's tears.

The Father does not become "unglued" by our tears. How could he? They are as much a part of his design as our hands and our feet.

We need never fear one word of condemnation from the Father—"Quit crying! Now!" Tears in failure, in grief, in disappointment, do not offend him.

Some of us find this difficult to accept because we have never had a parent demonstrate an acceptance of tears. The Lord gives us permission to cry. Our future need not be determined by our past.

God gives us the freedom to cry. If he has made us to cry, if he has, by the witness of the Word, seen the tears of saints, pilgrims, and sinners throughout history, he surely sees our tears.

It's OK to cry.

2
THE ANATOMY OF A TEAR

"Oh, that my head were a spring of water and my eyes a fountain of tears," the prophet Jeremiah lamented (9:1). Many of us have felt the same way at times. Although Jeremiah was a prophet and not a biologist, he was accurate. Scientists have discovered the headwaters of tears.

Take your hand and place it on the outside of your eyebrow, either right or left. Now think of an almond. Press slightly on your eyebrow. Just behind it and slightly above your eyeball lies the lacrimal gland—the womb of tears, the "fountain" in Jeremiah's words. Each gland has six to twelve lacrimal ducts through which the tears pass to arrive on the surface of your eyeball, the "stage" of the emotions.

Tears seem so simple—yet they are controlled by one of the most intricate mechanisms of the body. Obviously our Creator designed us to cry.

WHAT IS A TEAR?

Technically tears are lacrimal secretions, but that sounds too clinical. A tear is more than a thousand words.

Poets have acknowledged tears as the universal language of the soul. Every tribe, every culture has tears—although there is infinite variety in their explanation and acceptance.

To be precise, tears are "a dilute solution of various salts in water, containing small qualities of mucin"[1] or mucroproteins which in turn contain polysaccharides. Having said all that, a tear is 98 percent water.

In *The Miracle of Vision*, Dr. Arthur Freese praises the complex yet exact architecture of tears. Tears have three layers:

1. an inner mucous layer containing sodium chloride and sodium bicarbonate; which is surrounded by
2. tear water; and
3. an outer oily, filmy layer which lessens evaporation.[2]

However, the miraculous ingredient of a tear is a tiny enzyme called lysozyme, which was first identified by Sir Arthur Flemming, who also discovered penicillin. Lysozyme is a basic protein that is also found in egg white and in saliva. In the eye, its task is to keep the eye free of infection.

Lysozyme dissolves the protective outer coating of potentially threatening bacteria; you could say it disarms them the way western sheriffs took the guns of bandits. Ironically, lysozyme as a germ killer is stronger than carbolic acid, yet is completely harmless to the delicate tissues of the eye.[3] Again, it is a testimony to the genius of our Creator. "I am fearfully and wonderfully made" (Ps. 139:14).

WHAT IS THE PURPOSE OF TEARS?

The eye is such a delicate mechanism that intricate details were developed to protect its abilities. The first line of defense is, of course, the eyelids—upper and lower—which can close in a split second. But how do they glide over the delicate tissues of the cornea without causing friction and damage? The tear acts as a lubricant so that the eyelid literally "slides" over the surface of the eye.

Not all animals have eyelids; for example, snakes do not. Some species of birds, however, have three eyelids to guard against dust, sand, and twigs. Most birds never close their upper or lower eyelids but rely on a third set. Ducks and some species of birds have a goggle-like lens in this third eyelid which allows them to switch the focus of their eyes as they dive underwater searching for food. The other lenses are too farsighted from flying to enable the duck to identify objects at a close range.[4]

Without our awareness, tears flow continually in their assignment to keep the eye relatively clear of dust and microrganisms. The process pauses only as we sleep. That's why our eyes may be bloodshot when we first awaken. It takes fifteen to thirty seconds for the lysozyme to whiten the eyeball (its secondary function).

Dr. Ben Esterman calls tears "the world's oldest windshield wipers" (and probably the most effective, as well). Tears do not respond to gravity as we would assume but are directed across the eyes by the suction of the tear sac, the same muscle that causes the eye to blink. So each blink literally "mops the cleansing fluids in the tears across your eyes."[5]

Professor Marcel Monnier of the University of Basel in Switzerland adds two other functions. Tears prevent the cooling down of the corneal surface and also help the transparency of the cornea.[6] If you have ever driven with a dirty windshield you understand that principle. The tears help keep the cornea "clean."

DOES EVERYONE HAVE TEARS?

Some people have an insufficient supply of tears, a condition generally associated with a deficiency of vitamin A. The condition, known as *xerophthalmia,* is corrected through eyedrops.

Babies do not tear until usually the fourth month. An infant is born without a fully developed lacrimal system, so the newborn baby generally cries without tears. Sometimes, the baby's lacrimal glands must be gently massaged.[7]

Some people produce fewer tears after age fifty. Some adults suffer from Sjögren syndrome (90 percent of the victims are female), which damages the lacrimal glands. Those affected suffer painful burning, itching, and redness as well as a sensitivity to light. One woman reported it was like "having your eyes full of sand." In extreme cases, ulcers form on the cornea. Freese described one California woman who must wear thick aviator goggles at all times to protect her eyes.[8]

In an age of acute air pollution, tears will become even more valuable as a protective mechanism. However, there will be an increased use of over-the-counter eyedrops.

WHAT MOTIVATES TEARS?

There are three varieties of tears.

Functional tears result from an involuntary response and work to keep the surface of the eye free from dust, bacteria, and so on.

Reflex tears are a response to an immediate irritant, that is, when something "gets into your eye." Immediately the lacrimals release an extra regiment of tears to go to work removing the irritant. (This is not unlike the summoning of a fire engine to an accident in which gasoline has been spilled on a highway.) Other body functions stimulate reflex tears: sneezing, coughing, vomiting, choking, and certain types of hot spicy foods. Peeling onions may produce immediate tears.

Emotional tears (the major focus of this book) are produced by psychological stimulus: fear, anger, pain, or love. The cranial nerves (which control tear production) can be anesthetized and the first type of tears will be reduced, the second eliminated, but the tears of emotion will continue to flow.[9] It is safe to conclude that so committed to our tear-ability was the Creator that the pump is continually primed, ready to go into action on a moment's notice.

WHAT IS THE DIFFERENCE BETWEEN "TEARING" AND "CRYING"?

We use two different terms for the same physiological process—*tearing* and *crying.* However, one serves an important cultural process. Because of the stigma of crying in our culture, we need to differentiate between those tears caused by the emotions and those caused by reflex or function.

When one sheds tears due to emotion, the process is called *crying.*

When one sheds tears due to a reflex action (a slap across the face or peeling onions), the process is called *tearing.*

The Creator designed that the two be distinctive, and our culture has taken it a step further. Thus, a 260-pound steelworker would generally not cry during an argument but might "tear" while peeling onions to make homemade chili or at a particularly humorous joke he heard during his lunch hour.

WHAT HAPPENS TO TEARS AFTER THEY FALL?

Normally, tears are pumped across the surface of the eyes and into the tear sac through two tiny lacrimal ducts. The sac empties into the nasolacrimal duct and then into the nasal cavity. That's why crying causes the nose to run. There are too many "used" tears; it's like water that stands on the ground after a hard rain.

We might expect tears to flow downward due to the effect of gravity and thus spill over the lower eyelid, and they do during emotion-oriented crying. Jeremiah observed, "Our eyes overfow with tears and water streams from our eyelids" (Jer. 9:18).

Just as rivers and creeks, during times of flooding, can have water diverted or contained through sandbagging, so the eye has a similar process. If you pull back your lower eyelid you will discover a row of tiny yellowing dots. They are the openings for a group of glands embedded in the lower lid. Each of the thirty glands produces droplets of oil which coat the surface of the eyelid and act as a barricade to block the gravitational flow of tears. Tears created by functional or reflex situations flow into the tear sacs (and thus go unnoticed) rather than down our cheeks.[10]

Why don't the little glands just cooperate by creating more oil during a time of emotional crisis? Because we're designed to cry. If the emotional tears could be diverted or hidden, we would not signal our need of a tear-catcher.

Have you ever noticed someone trying not to cry but to be very composed? One or two tears flow down the cheek. That can be a loud yet silent proclamation of internal pain or tension. A tear on the cheek is never an accident; tears do not have the power on their own to "leap over" the oil in a defiant act.

The tear which flows down the cheek is a statement that the body cannot deal with a situation or crisis. So that tear becomes an unmistakable invitation to those who admit the universality of tears. That's why "What's wrong?" is never a cliché. A person who sees the tears cannot legitimately say, "Well, how was I to know you were hurting?"

"You saw the tear!"

WHAT HAPPENS IF WE SQUELCH TEARS?

If we were designed to breathe
   and chose not to
   we would die. It's that simple.
When the heart, designed to pump blood,
   stops, we die. It's that simple.
When the brain, designed to coordinate
   the body functions, ceases,
   we die. It's that simple.
When the tear process,
   as intricately designed by the Creator
   and ordained as the other "systems,"
   dies out,
   we pride ourselves on our self-control.
We are designed to weep, to cry,
   to visibly express ourselves
   as we are to breathe
      to think
      to talk
      to have a heartbeat.

Whenever a human decides to immobilize or over-discipline the tear process, a part of him or her dies. If you wrapped your right hand to your side or put your fingers into a cast, it would not be long before that particular body part would lose some of its function.

> One who has no tears
>   will soon have no heartbeat.
> Tears are the lowest common denominator
>   of humankind.

3

THE MOTIVATION OF A TEAR

Though we cannot always verbalize it, there is always a reason for tears. Children quickly ask "Why is he/she crying?" Sometimes a parent's answer satisfies the curiosity, but there must be times the answers trigger unasked questions. Why do people cry? An old song of the sixties noted "You would cry too if it happened to you!"

PEOPLE CRY BECAUSE OF PHYSICAL PAIN

One of the ways we learned about our world was that we hurt and then cried. That's why parents spank children. Remember that slogan, "Spare the rod, spoil the child"? The tears coupled with the child's desire to avoid pain and embarrassment will result in good (or tolerable) behavior as defined by their parents (but not necessarily by observers).

Most children cry when spanked. Some cry quickly; others cry reluctantly. Tears can short-circuit the punishment especially for a child who has a parent who remarks, "This hurts *me* more than it hurts you!" Some children stubbornly reserve their tears to further frustrate the parent.

Children quickly learn that adults in general (and grandparents in particular) become "unglued" with tears, and they learn to use tears to manipulate adults. Most parents will promise anything to avoid a crying tantrum in a department store. So a child may test the resolve of the parent, although a "just-wait-till-I-get-you-home" through clenched teeth can spell doom.

However, a pan of boiling water accidentally knocked over will produce tears as surely as will a spill from a tricycle. In many physical situations, the parent will say, "Didn't Mommy tell you that would hurt?" Through tears the child must admit that Mom was right *again*. Parents teach through tears.

Children also learn early that it's not OK to cry. Watch a child take a spill from a speedy tricycle. The child is initially stunned and looks to an adult for approval to cry. In many instances, a parent's reassurance "You're all right" prevents the tears; with other children, a physical embrace and a cookie will chase away the tears.

How many times were you promised a special treat *if* you wouldn't cry at the doctor's or dentist's office? Sometimes we struggled to keep the tears from flowing lest we lose the promised reward. Often we really wanted to cry. In those moments we looked to our parent(s) and reported (sometimes in a shaky voice), "I didn't cry."

Teasing children because of tears can set a dangerous precedent because it rewards the habit of ignoring physical or emotional pain. And it must be confusing for a child to be denied permission to cry (or be labeled "crybaby") but then to see adults crying without punishment.

It is clear that we teach children early that it is permissible (if not expected) for females to cry but unacceptable for males. Little boys are repeatedly told by authority figures (and by peers), "Big boys don't cry!" Therefore, if you cry you are *not* a big boy.

These childhood tapes continue to play throughout our lives.

PEOPLE CRY BECAUSE OF EMOTIONAL PAIN

As we mature we gain ways of dealing with pain. Thus a woman who might have cried from a doctor's injection as a little girl might only wince twenty-five years later. Now, however, she may cry after a thoughtless remark from her husband or a reprimand from an employer. As adults we are much more tolerant of physical pain than of emotional pain.

On the other hand, a colleague of mine has studied the responses from members of his congregation to a pastoral invitation for prayer requests. He discovered that we readily accept physical needs (headaches are easier to deal with than heartaches). Almost every request for prayer concerned a physical condition. But it was obvious that some individuals through psychosomatic influences camouflaged their emotional pains to receive the support they believed they needed.

PEOPLE CRY BECAUSE OF DELAYED EMOTIONAL PAIN

From conditioning and encouraged by pride, some people may not wish to cry in public. So they delay the tears until they can find a "safe" place. Today we often flee to the safety of a bedroom or a bathroom (where running water can drown out the sounds of crying). During my divorce, I recall many times that I cried while driving my car. That was my safe place.

Such a pattern is initiated in childhood when we are ordered, "Go to your room! I don't want to hear that crying!" Children learn to cry in isolation. We adults cannot always retreat to our rooms, so we learn to cry within the caverns of the soul.

A single parent shared the story of her son's modeling the anti-crying attitudes of his father. One day the child said to his grandmother, "Granny, I've learned how to do something that's really important."

"What is that?" the grandmother asked.

"I've learned how to cry in my brain so no one can see!" His beaming little face asked to be rewarded, but the grandmother could not.

Many people remarked about Jackie Kennedy's stamina and her resolve not to cry in public after President Kennedy's assassination. Many heralded her deportment as a heroic virtue. But there must have been some time when she wept.

Tear-catchers have an ability to gently discount the protests of the tear-sharer and give permission to cry. "Go ahead and cry; you'll feel better" is a way of saying "I won't think any less of you if you do cry."

Others have learned to cry quickly; parents would permit crying only for a brief period. Then we would hear a stern "That's enough!"

PEOPLE CRY FROM DELAYED TRAUMA

A young executive, known for her poise under pressure, had an automobile accident after she ignored posted warning signals. A policeman read her the riot act and she listened patiently. Later, in the safety of her condo, she wept hysterically as she recalled his lecture.

Many take-charge persons control their emotions to help others; so they clamp down on the tear sphincters during an illness, a funeral, or an argument. It may happen that later, in an unfolding awareness of how close they came to death or catastrophe, the tearflow erupts with volcanolike intensity.

PEOPLE CRY FROM EMOTIONAL RELEASE

When the jury returns the "not guilty" verdict, the defendant accused of murder, who has so long protested his innocence, breaks into tears. We weep when the doctor reports that the lump removed from a breast is *not* malignant or that an injured relative is going to be all right. Tears are an emotional release.

This is particularly the case with many religious people who summon their spiritual resources and say, "I've [or we've] got to be strong." Others, particularly men, insist that we flex our spiritual muscles and "take it like a man!" Some Christians reject crying as a sign of weak faith. Others suggest, "There's plenty of time for that later!" We cannot be strong all the time, and eventually the tears come.

PEOPLE CRY BECAUSE OF
EMOTIONAL UNCERTAINTY

When my father required hospitalization during a serious illness, my mother cried repeatedly and asked, "How will I live without your daddy?" I was put on the spot. Any agreement with her hopelessness in that moment would not have encouraged her to exercise faith. Yet a declaration, "You'll make it somehow" seemed a negation of my faith that he would live through the illness.

In many traumas we are overwhelmed with the "what if's." Because we cannot gaze into the crystal ball, we cry. Tears become a release from the tyranny of the unknown. This offers the tear-catcher an invitation to respond, with the assurance that everything is going to be all right, and with the reminder to trust God's love. Other tear-catchers choose to touch the person because a physical affirmation reinforces the warmth of the verbal communication.

We may encourage them to "eat something; you'll need your strength," although "whatever happens" may be understood but also unspoken.

The Jews hung up their harps and cried when they remembered Zion. Although they often sang in distress, they were now silent. In the uncertainty of the captivity of Babylon, the very thought of all they had taken for granted in Jerusalem deeply troubled them.

At a funeral, the recall of selective memories of the deceased in certain situations may produce a wave of new tears. This is one bittersweet function of visiting the bereaved. We take comfort in the memory of other, warmer days and a moment of appreciation for facets of the deceased's personality.

PEOPLE CRY FOR NO REASON AT ALL

Sometimes we cry "just 'cause" as they say down South. If we do not fully understand the motivations, we may confuse them. Culturally it is far more permissible for children or women to cry. Women in particular are freed from emotional limitations. Men respond, "Isn't that just like a woman?" or plead, "Please don't start crying on me."

Some women do cry more frequently during certain points of the menstrual cycle, in the period immediately following childbirth (the postpartum depression), or during menopause.[1] In such moments, tears assume a social function. A woman may be unable to tell her husband that she's depressed; tears communicate the need so that he can ask, "Honey, what's wrong?" (with sensitive husbands) or "What's wrong *now*?" (with insensitive mates). Tears attract attention and signal internal distress.

So some people cry as a symptom of their emotional status. Those married to a noncrier or strict emotional disciplinarian may be humiliated by their mate's inability to understand their tears. Parents too are often frustrated here. They want the child to stop crying long enough to discover the cause of the tears, but some children cannot comply long enough to fully explain. If the parent insists the crying stop "now," the child may perceive the parent as uncaring or unconcerned.

A good cry does make things better. That statement may not rest well under a microscope or analysis, but the history and tradition of humankind (and the personal experience of millions) testify to that slogan's validity.

Some people, however, have become so conditioned to crying as a way to communicate that they have failed to develop other avenues. On the other hand, so many people have an underdeveloped ability to cry that they cannot understand another's tears.

Most people would agree that tears are sometimes appropriate; the difficulty comes in agreeing at what point. When is a tear acceptable?

PEOPLE CRY IN THE BITTERSWEET EXPERIENCES OF LIFE

We may cry not because of the experience per se but rather from the internalized implications.

Notice the mother of the bride crying softly during her daughter's wedding (or the father becoming teary). The parents are happy—a beautiful day going according to intricately designed plans, a fantastic son-in-law who loves their daughter . . . yet, pain!

Notice the couple leaving the college campus after enrolling their son. Now his room will only occasionally be occupied and the grocery bill will decline. The mother remembers the nights she tucked him into bed and shared a story, or the nights she chased away "monsters." Both parents recall the nights they lay awake waiting for the family car's familiar sound. Where have all the years gone? That's the pain of the bittersweet.

Notice the man accepting fishing gear from his fellow employees; he doesn't feel old enough to retire. While he's longed for the days when he could really fish and hunt, the pain comes from the thirty-five years of habit—the habit of the familiar. Besides, how can these young guys really run the place without him? A gnawing suspicion is that they will.

Despite the preparing, the saving, the planning, somehow we're not ready to admit change, to make the necessary adjustments. The tears are in a sense a plea for a delay, "just a little more time."

PEOPLE CRY FROM SPIRITUAL FACTORS

Significant religious moments often produce tears. In some congregations, tears are the barometer of the effectiveness of the service.

I recall a prayer meeting when an older gentleman stood and said, "Pastor, I remember the good ole days. We used to have to bring two handkerchiefs to service." To which the pastor quickly responded, "Yes, one for blowing and one for showing."

While the pastor's response was a bit ironic, there was a period in American evangelical history when tears were common expressions of participants' involvement. I ran across an article not long ago about the evangelist Sam Jones, who conducted a tremendous revival campaign in the old Ryman Auditorium in Nashville, Tennessee (for many years the Grand Ole Opry House). He asked for everyone who wanted to go to heaven to "throw a hankie into the air." The reporter described the scene as thousands of handkerchiefs were thrown up and fluttered down.

As a child I had great difficulty reconciling the enthusiastic acceptance of tears in worship but their unacceptability at home. At church tears were a sign of spirituality. Mr. Phillips, for example, always cried aloud and "amened" the minister; Mrs. West frequently wiped tears during the service.

The ministers in my childhood memories always cried as they preached; on many occasions the congregation wept with a pastor in stereophonic coordination. Soloists occasionally wiped tears as they sang; some stopped to gain emotional control. We believed such moments were orchestrated by the Holy Spirit, although they could be faked. But most people knew the genuine as a jeweler can spot diamonds from glass synthetics despite the cut or sparkle.

Some people came to church "with the cups right-side-up," prepared to "expect a blessing." Prayer services before the main service served to prime the pump. Yet many of these people rejected (or even denounced) the "formality" of other churches. The ultimate praise of many pastors' sermons was "There wasn't a dry eye in the place!" What a compliment!

My tradition encouraged "sharing" in what was then called testimony meeting. Every Wednesday night the body gathered to sing, to pray, to study the Bible, but primarily to share. Many who testified spoke of personal or family struggles, of temptation, and of victory. Many ended, "Please remember me in your prayers." Sister Jones's problems with her alcoholic husband became a concern of the entire body of believers. The tears of a sharer evoked sympathetic and supportive tears from the congregation, particularly from those who had experienced the same temptation or problem. No one watched the clock in those days; we stayed until all minds were clear.

The significant spiritual moments of others (our children, our mates, close friends) touch the soul the way a harpist strums the tight strings on a harp. We are designed to participate in the anxieties of others.

Tears are an intricately learned spiritual shorthand facilitating for some people communion with God. In nature, the signature of God in a beautiful, crisp fall morning or a sunset over the Gulf of Mexico summons tears from sensitive pilgrims.

Imagine a performance of Handel's *Messiah* in which the chorus and orchestra are superb. The "Hallelujah Chorus" may bring enthusiastic applause from a secular audience yet tears in a church setting.

One of the floats in the 1981 inaugural parade carried the Mormon Tabernacle Choir. The float stopped in front of the presidential reviewing stand while the choir sang "The Battle Hymn of the Republic." President Reagan shed tears in that moment. And across America there were those who rejoiced in the performance. Although many had heard the song on other occasions, there was something about that moment that made tears appropriate; a profoundly moving experience.

WE ARE DESIGNED TO CRY

We are creatures designed and equipped to cry: the pump is primed, the reservoir is stockpiled, and there seems to be no shortage of occasions which provoke tears.

But there is a shortage of those persons willing to catch the tears. That surely is an aberration of the Creator's design. How could he have designed such an intricate process and interaction without a corresponding capacity within us to see tears as valuable and precious?

How can we praise as a virtue that self-control which causes us to become disinterested spectators in the presence of genuine crying? Helmuth Plessner observed,

"More forcefully than any other expressive pattern or emotion, the crying of our fellowman grips us and makes us partners of his moment, often, 'without even knowing why.' "[2]

The attention on physical fitness, jogging, health foods, mental wholeness may encourage a generation willing to freely accept tears—a generation who will celebrate tears could change history!

Ironically, such a generation may well reduce the actual number of tears shed by normalizing a process so long viewed as suspect or unnatural. When I enjoy the freedom to cry without stigma, I will find other means to communicate.

In that event, we will have made a gigantic stride toward the wholeness God beckons us to discover. If the Father was not embarrassed by Jesus' tears, why should mine be condemned?

4

THE REGIMENT OF SPECTATORS

Why do we need tear-catchers? We have an army of psychologists, psychiatrists, and therapists, all trained, credentialed. Today it's as normal to go to a counselor as to a dentist. In some circles, one's therapist's advice is considered appropriate after-dinner conversation. Pop psychology and how-to books overflow the shelves of mall bookstores as well as nightstands at every level of society. And what TV talk show could be successful without a "people helper" interacting with the latest Las Vegas routine?

How did we get this way?

THE ME GENERATION

That Pepsi generation which danced its way across our televisions and into our consciousness has had a major theological impact. This is the era of the first person singular.

"I've got to be me," has become the official anthem of the movement. In an era of overemphasis on youth and looking young and a phobia of aging (just notice the advertising fixation on constipation, dentures, and hemorrhoids), we're almost psychologically paralyzed.

At the same time there is a sting to the remark, "You're acting like a kid." I recently overheard two women commenting on a man, and one responded, "Oh, he's forty-five going on seventeen."

One aspect is the impact of the mid-life crisis. A businessman wakes up and says, "I'm getting old . . . and I don't want to be *old*." So he begins to act out a second adolescence.

Perhaps all the commotion began with a generation who could not say the word *no* to its offspring. Members of this generation wanted to "make it up to" their children. To deny a child anything was commonly judged malfeasance of parenthood. So *no* atrophied and there were no acceptable synonyms. Therefore, a new generation so trained is trying to parent with an essential ingredient for successful parenting sadly lacking: *no*.

A decade ago we protested about offensive four-letter words; today we decry the offensive two letters: *n-o!* Many children were taught not to take *no* seriously; *no* was always negotiable. Children learned a parent's "no" to their request (or demand) to ride the horsey outside a department store could be negotiated with any number of behaviors: charm, tears, a 1- 2- or 3-star tantrum, or a combination of all these.

The deletion of *no* from a priority position in our vocabulary has weakened the entire language and the society as well.

And if nothing should be rejected, we want it yesterday. We have become an instant people: we want our needs met *now*. So we take two cups of cold milk, add instant pudding mix, stir vigorously for two minutes, and there you have pudding "as good as grandmother used to make," according to the ads (but not the taste buds and memories). This preoccupation with the instant carries over into the world of the spiritual as well.

We want instant relationships and friendships. "Old Harry's my buddy," and Harry hardly knows you. We don't have time to cultivate relationships. Magazines and talk-show guests have reduced intimacy to its lowest common denominator: sex. Even the Christian world has gotten swept into the tide.

Besides, if we spend time developing relationships and friendships, what if they move across the country? Consider the choices:

1. Don't get attached.
2. Attach immediately; enjoy it while it lasts.
3. Keep the relationship on surface level.

The Cult of the Me has spiritualized the passage, "I can do everything through him who gives *me* strength" (Phil. 4:13, italics mine). We know how to emphasize the first person singular when sharing. I've been in sharing sessions where Philippians 4:13 resembled a portable neon sign, blinking out its "I" message to listeners. And how can we respond but with a rousing "Praise the Lord"?

The Cult of the Me has its origins with the first human beings. When God confronted Adam and asked, "Where are you?" Adam responded, "I heard you in the garden, and I was afraid because I was naked; so I hid" (Gen. 3:10). Adam certainly liked the use of *I* to use it four times in his answer.

But his son inherited the me-fixation. When God confronted Cain, he responded, "Am I my brother's keeper?" (Gen. 4:9). God's answer then *and now* is yes. In the Cult of the Me, however, we define who is our neighbor. And my neighbor is probably a lot like me.

The Cult of the Me is heavily influenced by our fixation with youth. We have attempted to entertain this generation with a cadre of youth ministers, many of whom are little more than kids themselves. Oddly, when we forsook the family doctor for the specialist, we paralleled that decision in the church. We gave our children over to youth ministers, a significant portion of whom have meager theological training. In essence, we are turning over our most valued resource to the least experienced. Would a diamond company turn the Hope diamond over to a novice cutter? Never.

Kenneth Gangel warned a conference of church leaders of the danger of a generation of specialists who are "good with youth" but lack resources in Bible, theology, and counseling. As churches have become more affluent, the paid associates, particularly in youth, have become a status symbol. For too many it has been purchasing a type of "spiritual babysitting."

As a result of this youth fixation and program orientation, we have developed a shortage of young men and women ready to move into the adult world. Many have entered adulthood with this mentality: design a program *for me*!

And the church is a victim of its own logic.

THE SPECTATOR/THE SPECTACLE

"Can you top this?" seems to be a common thrust of ministry. We like fads; we seem fascinated by the new. We're into programs and their newest synonym: ministries. Go to a seminar and listen to the presentation; take good notes.

If the material is not copyrighted, half a dozen will take the materials and graft them to an already existing program. (If the material is copyrighted, permission from the copyright owner must be obtained before it can be used.) Imitations will spring up overnight; some way, the hours of slow evolvement and development are erased.

But it is in the hours of developing a program idea that a bond of confidence emerges between those who need the program and those who are responding creatively to the need. I had the pleasure to work with SALT I, the Single Adult Leadership Training Conference in Dallas in 1980. This was the first forum for bringing together single adult leaders from across the country. What happened, though, was that the six originators of the conference became deeply involved in one another's lives. That was worth more for us than any program and continues to affect our lives.

Today's church is producing too many spectators in assembly-line fashion. Juan Carlos Ortiz, the Argentine evangelist, noted the church is not growing but rather is "getting fat." Despite the growth of his congregation, he concluded, "We only multiplied more babies." Ortiz discovered he was not pastoring a church but running a spiritual orphanage.[1]

Look at our programs which naturally attract people. I have many friends who are ministers or directors of music. Each summer they begin frantically searching for a new Christmas musical to top last year's. Without regard to a choir's ability or discipline, some still look over the fence into their neighbor's choir loft. "Wow, First Church did that musical and had a thousand people three nights in a row." Let one church have a singing Christmas tree, and next year in that community there will be a half-dozen scaled-down imitations.

The temptation is to attempt the spectacular. "Now, that's the way to put our church on the evangelical map of our city." And we find a way to spiritualize it all, including the expense. We want to one-up our competition the way grocery stores do.

As a result, a host of music ministers (and their families) hate the Christmas season because they know they *have* to top last year's program and "hype" their choir members past stretching to accomplish the goal. And the robes are hardly back in the rack before it's time to start thinking about Easter.

But people see the fantastic on Sunday morning television, once the programming ghetto, now the evangelical version of prime time. In the electronic church, the minister never has a bad sermon, an off day; the choir's always on pitch; the soloist and accompanist are always in the same key. All work to create a flawless performance.

When people have been exposed to that while eating Sunday breakfast or getting dressed to come to church, they are spoiled. Thus our worship experiences are becoming more production oriented. And that takes a lot of energy. So the layperson asks, why be overworked in a smaller church where I am expected to

- sing in the choir
- teach a Sunday school class
- take a turn in the nursery
- bake three dozen cookies for the teen party
- serve on the missionary council
- open my pocketbook to the needs of the church?

Why do that when I can go to a large church and sit back and enjoy the service, orchestrated by a skilled staff of professionals who work hard to pull it all off?

I got a letter on a church's stationery the other day, and the whole left-hand side of the paper was taken up by the names of the paid ministers of the church.

But a spectator church does not train tear-catchers.

WEARY IN WELL-DOING

Some people have become weary in well-doing or overinvolvement. "Be good to yourself" is a growing cliché. So some churches have designed a recruitment system that resembles a candy machine. "Step right up, folks, and pick out what appeals to you. Look at the great selections." It is like a candy fanatic checking out all the potential offerings. So you put in your quarter, press the number corresponding to your selection, then pick up the blessing below.

Too often the church workers are so busy organizing programs and picnics and all-night roller skating parties and cantatas and showers and curriculum review sessions that they don't have time for real ministry or to catch tears. Sometimes in moments of exhaustion and frustration they covet the pew-sitter's sit-back-and-watch approach. When the hours of "thankless," unappreciated giving mount up and that moment when they need a breather finally comes, they practically have to beg for relief.

Every so often we have those great "Joe Jones Appreciation Sundays" and everyone feels less guilty but hardly more inspired to get involved. I believe this is a carryover from our culture. "What's the use?" or "Is that all the thanks I get?" It doesn't help when someone hogs the credit—after all, the church is still full of humans.

There was once a period of time when we could sing enthusiastically, "This world is not my home, I'm just a passin' through." The church seemed a safe enclave from societal problems. However, now we're faced with the awareness that the answerless dilemmas of our society are also found in the church. We turn our backs on the problems we see on the six o'clock news and yet wonder why we don't sing "I'll Fly Away" anymore.

But the members of the first-century church took a different approach. They tackled the problems of their day. Do we need Paul's instructions on caring for widows and orphans when we have Social Security and Aid to Dependent Children (and legions of paperwork and bureaucracy and miles of red tape) for those who need it?

What would we do with Ruth and Naomi today? Ruth seems such an embarrassment to the Cult of the Me. Unlike Orpah, her sister-in-law, Ruth gave up everything (her people, her gods, her country) to care for her mother-in-law. That seems unwise by today's standards. Her proclamation, "May the Lord deal with me, be it ever so severely, if anything but death [no loopholes] separates you and me" (Ruth 1:17) seems a bit too dramatic.

She toiled day after day harvesting barley in Boaz's fields to get enough food to keep herself and Naomi alive. Yet with no economic structures (Social Security, pension, insurance) the society through leverate law provided hope for these widows.

Two generations later, Ruth's grandson sat as king of Israel—an incredible return on her investment of kindness. God can still do that—but we are weary of involvement. Let the widow, let the single parent talk to a trained, credentialed social worker. Let the government do it—that's what we pay taxes for!

ANSWERLESS DILEMMAS

Our confidence has been assaulted. Who's confident to do anything anymore? It began in the home when mother's intuition gave way to pediatricians (predominantly males), whose fathering experience (due to the demands of their practice) was primarily biological and economic.

Then we developed hordes of specialists, consultants, advisors. One would have thought that with our knowledge we could have orchestrated a solution to most problems. We can take abstract physics and mathematics and help a man walk on the moon, but we can't walk safely downtown in most of our cities at midnight. If a cure for cancer were discovered tomorrow, we would have to invent a new disease. Just how many incurable diseases were there a generation ago before we started the massive telethons to raise millions for research? We're walking pharmacies; yet we criticize the drug dependencies of our youth.

We've looked for a political messiah to rescue us nationally but have chosen to ignore the prophets who have always shared equal billing in God's design. The feeling persists that our problems are too enormous. Thus we suffer a collective hopelessness. You take the individual's feelings and multiply by the census and you have a composite fear and paralysis.

Yet we are ruthless on the applicants for the leadership roles. In 1972, we eliminated one candidate when he wept during the New Hampshire primary. How could he lead us?

The real leaders, who might well be able to solve our problems and create a new wave of confidence in government and Yankee ingenuity, may be too wise to step into the arena. How quickly we become disenchanted with those we do elect!

We have run through the dilemma solvers, yet the mood persists that our problem is too big. Meanwhile, we are impatiently hungry for an immediate but painless answer. We want solutions that require no risk, no sacrifice. Perhaps on someone else's part, but certainly not on mine.

Social Security is a good "for instance." Everyone believes in Social Security—it's like baseball and apple pie. And with gray power now a political reality, we are more conscious of the older voter. So Congress periodically votes through higher monthly payments *and deductions*. Social Security taxes have increased dramatically in the last ten years.

Each increase means that I take home less. Now I cannot complain too loudly because my parents receive Social Security but I (along with millions of others my age and younger) am wondering, Is there going to be anything left for me when I retire?

Our nation has fought an incredible battle with inflation, yet a slight percentage increase in deductions, such as the raise in 1981 from 6.13 percent to 6.75 percent, removed $16 billion annually from the economy—money people would have spent in stores and shops. That's one example of merry-go-round economics; indeed, an answerless dilemma.

Consider the fuel shortage. We all agree we need to reduce the amount of gasoline consumed—if just to reduce our dependency on Arabian oil. But I still want to be able to drive my car *anytime* and *anywhere* I please (and at more than 55 m.p.h.). That's my right, you know. Yet we forget there is only a certain amount of oil left in the world—and when that is gone there is no more.

A skin diver knows there is only a certain number of minutes of oxygen in his tanks. He can swim anywhere he wants—but when the oxygen is gone, the oxygen is gone. There will be consequences to his decision. He cannot recapture the expended oxygen. In fact, he can endanger his life by accidentally miscalculating. Nature can be most uncooperative.

So the answerless dilemmas of our culture have become the answerless dilemmas of our communities, our churches, our homes, and our spirits.

We're struggling for an antidote, a cure for our addiction to first person singular (or plural) living. If we could put the dilemmas on the back burner long enough to catch our breath, we might discover an answer. It's not unlike the harried businessman who is on the phone and sees all the incoming lines blinking "on hold," demanding to be answered. Which call does he take next?

We're weary of solutions that unravel or bend or fray under pressure. We demand steel for tin prices; a Cadillac for Volkswagen payments. For some, the only sane answer is to desensitize the walls of the spirit—to tune out, to escape.

Our hopelessness and lack of confidence in our abilities keep the seminar business going and how-to authors speaking and writing. Our desperation—our panic— sends us to some questionable sources, just as Saul sought out the witch at Endor.

The evangelical church has struggled with its work- manship; we're lost in our pluralness. We're trying to hang on to the bucking horse of success. Evangelicals have arrived. But the problems seem to sneer at us. And we sigh as did the Jews, "How shall we sing the Lord's song in a strange land?"

ANYONE NEED A GOOD TEAR-CATCHER?
NO EXPERIENCE NEEDED!

Into this arena steps the tear-catcher. Not as a Pollyanna prophet nor as someone with head so deeply embedded in the sand as to be unable to smell the stench of hell, of defeat, of alienation.

> Tear-catchers know
> all about the ME age
> of the weariness of involvement
> of the answerless dilemmas

because they have struggled with them before and will face them again. They pride themselves not on victory *over* these factors but in surviving the grip of their tight tentacles.

Tear-catchers cannot sit with their friends in the quiet of the sidelines or in the safety of the grandstands. Tear-catchers are player-coaches.

Their only salvation in the moment when the natural inclination would be to flee is that they know *whose* they are and therefore know who they are! So they can listen to the doubter, the cynic, fully aware of their own doubts, concerns, and fears. And they can comfort those who weep without demanding immediate gratification. Tear-catchers can survive because they believe in tomorrow. In searching for a calculated balance of these factors, they find strength. The folly of many would-be tear-catchers is to ignore factors rather than become disciplined by placing them in perspective.

There will be times when these factors will regroup to mount another offensive; they seldom just go away. But one helpful quality is persistence. Chuck Swindoll has written a powerful book on perseverance through pressure: *Three Steps Forward, Two Steps Back.* His conclusion is simple: "We're all faced with a series of great opportunities brilliantly disguised as impossible situations."[2]

Tear-catchers do not have the luxury of "off the top of the head" solutions. Tear-catchers are aware of how resistant the problems may be. They do not fear the taunt of hopelessness or the jeer of helplessness—they fear the enemy in themselves: overconfidence, a smugness that paralyzes.

> Because he can never forget that moment
> of his aloneness
> when he cried
> The tear-catcher reaches out
> to others whose now
> resembles his yesterday.

Simply, there is no shortage of situations that produce tears. Rather, the shortage seems to be of those who would catch them.

A tear-catcher is someone
   who accepts, and
   occasionally encourages
   another's tears
   as a treasured gift.
A tear-catcher does not judge
   the cause of the tears
   or the one who shares them.
Most of the time,
   he will not ask the why
   but accepts tears
   as a guest accepts
   one's hospitality.

5

CALL OUT THE MILITIA

Something's wrong, somewhere.

- Christians have made the covers of *Time*.
- George Gallup samples evangelicals for their opinions.
- Christian ministries are springing up all over.
- Many pastors are returning for advanced training, particularly through the doctor of ministry degree programs.
- The born-again movement produces raw new recruits every day.
- Never have we had so many skilled professionals or people-helpers.

Yet in the enthusiasm of the born-again movement, there exists a brooding silence:

- a housewife whose husband ignores her
- a husband whose marriage is stale
- a person hiding in an emotional closet

- a promiscuous teen, wondering why she still feels so lonely after sex
- Social Security recipients, counting pennies, wondering if their sons and daughters will come to visit
- a victim of child abuse whose wounds never heal before the next beating
- the parents locked into an economic rat race who provide their children with "things" as a compensation for time
- the parents who are shattered by the drug dependency of their daughter or the homosexuality of their son
- the ne'er-do-well who longs for success and promises, "This time things are gonna work out"
- those who have become disillusioned with the church

And yet people ask, "Why do we need tear-catchers?"

We need tear-catchers because the need for them exists. People weep themselves to sleep at night; many struggle with unwept tears. Despite the legions of ordained clergy and thousands of candidates for ordination studying in theological seminaries, we're just scratching the surface. We also need tear-catchers because pastors cry too. Tear-catching cannot be structured into a theological or health-professional curriculum. Indeed, some professors would question the existence of such a discipline as just another fad.

Over the past years, nations have expanded the use of special forces to engage in guerilla warfare. These trainees reject the comfort of the barracks for the front line.

The church over the same years has developed a militia of ministers, many of whom are permanent residents of the barracks. In today's world, those who want to minister to people's needs may have to abandon the safety of the barracks.

I spent several years preparing for ordination in my denomination and have chosen not to complete the process. The only aspects of ministry that are not open to me are the administration of the sacraments and performing weddings. I am fulfilled as a layman.

My calling was shaped through my graduate work at Scarritt College in Nashville, Tennessee. Scarritt is one of only two colleges in the world designed to train laity for church service. Dr. Leonard Wolcott, who taught a course called "The Nature and Mission of the Church," had a fascination with II Corinthians 5:18-20; his interest became contagious.

> All this is from God, who reconciled us to himself through Christ *and gave us the ministry of reconciliation:* that God was reconciling the world to himself in Christ, not counting men's sins against them. And he has committed to us the message of reconciliation. We are therefore Christ's ambassadors, *as though God were making his appeal though us.* (italics mine)

"The ministry of reconciliation." That is the unique call to be a *tear-catcher*. A tear-catcher serves as an ambassador of Christ. If we understand that, we can understand Jesus' dilemma when those he selected to catch his tears in the dark shadows of Gethsemane fell asleep.

But why do we need tear-catchers when we have the ministerial militia?

THE ORDAINED MINISTRY IS OVERDEVELOPED

Despite recent advances in the recognition of the laity (and their stirring from hibernation), a notion persists that God has an elect, the ordained, and then the others, the laity. Therefore, those God "most" loves he calls into full-time Christian service. Such a notion, although most unbiblical, is fueled by those who missed opportunities for formal training and have ministered under an educational inferiority complex. That's not a new idea. Moses retorts to God who had called him to lead the Israelites: "O Lord, I have never been eloquent, neither in the past nor since you have spoken to your servant. I am slow of speech and tongue" (Exod. 4:10). We're never more biblical than when we reject ourselves for possible service. Many of us have passed on such feelings to our children. I know my grandmother Baker never thought she amounted to much because she did not go to India as a missionary.

A lot of laity have hungered or even coveted the call. Many, too many, have given up first-class lives as laity for frustrated service as ordained persons because they thought they were called.

Yet another group some would cruelly call "the deserters." These are the professional servants who have found the ordained ministry to be less than meaningful or have found ecclesiastical ladder-climbing or personal kingdom-building offensive and have become disillusioned.

Somehow, too many servants become lost in the politics of the church—and no denomination or independent work is immune; some simply have less sophisticated or informal bureaucracies. Increasingly, success in the ordained ministry is determined by the nonpriestly functions. The pastor has emerged as manager.

Management principles from the cutthroat world of business have been grafted into the lifestream of today's church. This process began harmlessly as businessmen on church governing boards began encouraging the consideration of business principles in church decision-making. But it was only a short hop to the illogical conclusion,

"What's good for General Motors is good for First Church!" and "All in favor say 'aye.' "

Some ministers, threatened by the potential intrusion into their world, chose to become "management specialists" as a way of controling their laity. Many preferred that the laity go organize a church softball league or bake sale and leave the controls of the church to the trained, called, ordained professionals.

Today, competition for recognition of expertise on the pages of evangelical magazines is important. Members of a church may be more pleased with their pastor's recognition as an administrator than as a prophet, particularly when their pastor is traveling the countryside converting disciples to his administrative philosophy.

Can a pastor catch a member's tears in Dallas and at the same time be in Chicago lecturing in a management conference? So what if the church gets exposure? The conclusion is, "Why, those people must really be something to have a great [or *great*] pastor like that." However, the next logical question is, "Wonder why our pastor doesn't have more on the ball?"

There are now an increasing number of church members (who happen to be paying the bills) who don't care if their pastor knows beans about management (they can hire a professional administrator for that). But can the pastor catch tears *and* be available while the tears are still warm?

Can you see a layman bringing in a tear-specimen to his pastor's office? "These are the tears I shed while you were gone."

The people who have paid the big bucks to get into the management sessions fail to realize that back at the ranch the overworked local church staff must compensate for their leader's absence by assuming significant portions of the work load, particularly counseling. Yet friends ask in soft tones, "What's HE like?" and the associates are ashamed to respond, "I don't know; he's never here!"

Can you imagine the great preachers of the past being touted as management specialists or administrators? A certain pastor was called to a large congregation because he could preach and because he was a tear-catcher. And he built a great church through great preaching.

There's another side to all this. People come to hear THE BIG MAN, yet they fail to penetrate his defenses. So the question is, who catches the BIG MAN's tears?

We will soon have to decide if the managerial dimension can be developed without sacrificing pastoral call. To many laypeople, a pastor's commitment to the managerial arena is confusing. If he's good, what's he doing here? He could be making a lot more money at General Motors.

Consider the disciples. The managerial specialist, Judas, ultimately betrayed Jesus, while the weak one, John, who lay on Jesus' breast, wrote a significant portion of the New Testament that has nourished pilgrims for nineteen hundred years.

The church does have to be a wise steward of its resources, but to overemphasize the economic aspect or continually overshadow the biblical model is risky. God calls people to be shepherds of the flock, not bureaucrats.

In our evangelical success, people are becoming fuel for the machinery. Perhaps before long *Fortune* will begin listing the TOP 500 CHURCHES—wouldn't that give a congregation status?

One pastor, Earl Lee of Pasadena First Church of the Nazarene, has publicly called for a moratorium on conferences so pastors can have more time to get work done where they draw their salaries.[1]

THE MINISTRY IS OVERSPECIALIZED

The general practitioner has become almost extinct in medicine because of the increase in specialized medicine. In a similar way the church today has so specialized its staff that they often do what laity *could* and *should* be doing. The laity is caught up with business and family and other commitments. Therefore, to insure that the job is done right, churches hire it done. Besides, associate positions under the shadow of a "super-pastor" seem a natural way to climb. Many churches gamble that the charisma rubs off on the novice.

It is possible through comprehensive theological education to know the biblical languages of Greek and Hebrew and yet miss the language of compassion. Gary Collins wrote in *Christianity Today* about the proliferation of self-helpers.

> The clearest message that comes from the Christian popularizers is that the local church has failed to show people how to apply their faith to the practical problems of life. . . . Maybe we should blame the seminaries for teaching a dead orthodoxy that leaves the graduate proficient in Greek and Hebrew but profoundly ignorant of basic human needs and interpersonal skills.[2]

Theological education focuses on the analytical, the logical, rather than on the caring, intuitive, sensitive. Too many seminary professors are out of touch with people's lives because their pastoral experiences are so far in the past or almost nonexistent.

As theological sophistication increased, the prominent divinity schools (Boston, Yale, Harvard, Vanderbilt, Chicago) influenced, in turn, the faculties in the denominational seminaries. "Publish or perish" became "Publish or parish" in many institutions of ministerial training.

Such a thing would never happen in medical education, where the classroom and the clinic go hand in hand.

There needs to be a process to regularly send seminary professors back into active parish ministry *if* they are going to train ministry practitioners.

Pastoral care cannot be practiced within stained-glass walls; not many tears are caught there because people who shed them cannot count on getting a good recommendation when they go looking for their first assignment.

Too many people have been graduated from seminaries and divinity schools with strong academic preparation: they know Bultman and Tillich and a lexicon of German theological terminology, but they do not understand the steelworker or the blue-collar worker or the nine-to-five worker fighting the monotony of the plant, the office, the factory.

Most laypeople really don't care about the mysteries of systematic theology; they want someone to wipe and catch their tears. They want someone to point them to tomorrow. They want someone to see hope in this vale of tears called life.

Too many have gone to have a pastor deal with a wound and have noticed the pastor wince as the bandage is lifted. In those moments, it is too easy to smooth down the bandage and go it alone.

With the expansion of paid professional staff (which in turn has increased the churches' payrolls), laypeople have been forced to confess their incompetence. In some cases, a layperson dare not question the staff member. Why, look on the wall at the neatly and attractively framed diplomas and degrees and certificates!

Yet people and their needs have been lost in the cracks. So they sit patiently in the congregation going through a cosmetic ritual (hoping the lines at the restaurant won't be too long), or they abandon the process entirely.

Others have joined the electronic congregations. OK, they admit it's "spiritual junk food" but the electronic church makes few demands on its members "out there in TV land." And it's a lot more comfortable in one's own living room than in the isolation of worship in a local church. But it's a two-way street.

> The old man in 312 never gets visitors.
> Oh, but he's so religious.
>   He sends money to
>   "Brother Bill's TV Ministry, Inc."
> But when the old man got sick
>   no one from "The Ministry"
>   phoned, sent flowers or visited.
> So, I did.
>   Maybe that's one difference
>   between an organization or
>   a nonprofit ministry
>   and a church.
> The old man in 312
>   whom I've never met before
>   becomes my brother.
> P.S.: But he'll still send a check
>   to Brother Bill
>   as soon as he's out of Room 312.

"Here's what needs to be done. Can you help?" becomes not an invitation to service but a threat. And on the other hand, some are too timid to even ask, "What can I do?" In too many settings, the approach is (1) convince the congregation of the need, and (2) suggest that *the* appropriate response is to financially underwrite the program and personnel. And for many pew-warmers, it is easier to reach for the checkbook than the day-to-day planner or calendar.

THE SYSTEM IS OVERTAXED BY THE CASUALTIES

Despite the abundance of trained, certified, competent shepherds, too many no longer feel comfortable with the system. Many configurations are led by networks of "good old boys"; the young man with ideas had better be careful of his initial allegiances. Tragically, some of our finest shepherds have burned out because they could not consciously meet all the demands. They went to the conferences on church growth and listened to the success stories. And sometimes they came home and turned a new leaf, but somehow the result was not as easy as the seminar leaders suggested.

We need tear-catchers for the tear-catchers. But most of them won't stand still long enough. Matthew observed: "When he saw the crowds, he had compassion on them, because they were . . . like sheep without a shepherd" (Matt. 9:36).

Why was Jesus needed, anyway? There were thousands of rabbis and priests and aides—an intricate ecclesiastical structure ranging from the office of the high priest and the esteemed doctors of the law. Yet people hurt.

Ezekiel's words seem appropriate. The word of the Lord came to him concerning the shepherds' failure to care for the flock. Listen to Ezekiel's writing:

> You have not strengthened the weak or healed the sick or bound up the injured. You have not brought back the strays or searched for the lost. You have ruled them harshly and brutally. So they were scattered because there was no shepherd, and when they were scattered they became food for all the wild animals. My sheep wandered over all the mountains and on every high hill. They were scattered over the whole earth, and no one searched or looked for them. (Ezek. 34:4-6)

Jesus came because the existing system was unworkable, insensitive, burdensome. Today, as our society continues its fixation with credentials and self-fulfillment, the army of strugglers and dropouts seeking help will multiply.

Somehow we must find a balance between the liberals and conservatives, the "do-gooders" and the "Bible quotin', Bible totin' " fundamentalists. The church has all but abandoned the poor—after all, we have the government. So the poor wait for a bureaucracy to help them. People for whom Jesus died become numbers and statistics and percentages to be governed by the rules and regulations and red tape.

And the human need intensifies.

Is the gospel silent on the treatment of the poor? Hardly. Concern for the poor is to spiritual health what oxygen is to the blood. What if Mary and Joseph had had to rely on the welfare system?

It is too easy for affluent, well-fed people to protest the system while "Amening" diatribes against welfare cheats. We have developed a folklore about people who couldn't buy dog food with their food stamps, so they bought steak for Rover instead.

Is it perhaps easier for a portion of our salary to be deducted to "provide for such people" through taxes than to personally become involved?

Have we ever thoroughly examined Jesus' finances? Would they bear the scrutiny of our biases? How *did* Jesus finance his ministry? Luke reported that as Jesus "traveled about from one city and village to another," some women helped support the disciples "out of their own means" (Luke 8:3).

Paul's example as a tentmaker has been used by some to question the paid-clergy concept. But note Paul's concern: "I have not coveted anyone's silver or gold or clothing. You yourselves know that these hands of mine have supplied my own needs and the needs of my companions. In everything I did, I showed you that by this kind of hard work we must help the weak" (Acts 20:33-35).

Overspecialization today is not limited just to the church—it's a part of our society's burden. Look at our massive and expensive educational system which, despite its cost and technology, still "produces" graduates who cannot read, compute, or think analytically to the point that many states are instituting twelfth-grade competency examinations in order to determine which students qualify for graduation.

Our penal system, despite more criminologists and counselors and expenditures, cannot rehabilitate a criminal and return him to society whole. Only recently has a new organization of tear-catchers led by Chuck Colson tackled the cold, brutal hells of incarceration.

The cult of individualism and the smorgasbord of self-helps have destroyed our human confidence and exhausted the wells of compassion.

So we struggle alone.

BUT WHAT CAN ONE PERSON DO?

What can one person do against such massive, complex problems? That old saying comes to mind, "The ocean is so big and my boat is so small." A host of burned-out casualties who thought they could make a difference confess that "nothing's going to change." Many do not have enough strength to add an exclamation point.

Yet the gospel insists that God and *one* person become a majority; God looks for people willing to take him at his word. Sometimes he ignores our protests. Despite Jeremiah's confessions, "I do not know how to speak; I am only a child" (Jer. 1:6), God continued to call him and his faithfulness to God did have an impact. Jesus told the disciples "You did not choose me, but I chose you" (John 15:16).

Jeremiah's protest "I am only a child" in today's vernacular is

- "I am only a housewife."
- "I am only an auto mechanic."
- "I am only an air-conditioning repairman."
- "I am only a factory worker."

We can string together what we might think is an impressive array of excuses. Consider the testimony of Amos.

> I was neither a prophet nor a prophet's son, but I was a shepherd, and I also took care of sycamore-fig trees. But the Lord took me from tending the flock and said to me, "Go, prophesy to my people Israel." (Amos 7:14-15)

If the Lord dismissed Jeremiah's self-doubt and Amos' lack of credentials and Moses' low self-image, he must dismiss all our well-worded doubts.

By one man's obedience (Joseph), Jesus was born in Bethlehem. If Joseph had not been willing to become involved in God's design (although he did not fully understand it) where would we be today?

One man, one woman, one child catching tears *can* make a difference.

There is a gentle stirring of the Spirit in our world today—summoning us from our boredom and restlessness into his adventure. He seeks those willing to abandon labels and credentials and "cloaks of expertise" in order to become servants.

In a paraphrase of Philippians 2:6-7:

> Although he was in nature God
>> he did not consider equality with God
>> something to be clasped tightly
>
> But made himself nothing
>> and took the very nature of a servant.

Are you willing to abandon

- the comfortable
- the convenient
- the "this is the life"
- the clear
- the safe

for a world where people weep, some audibly, others in silence? There is a place for you. There are those tears that only you can catch!

Despite the enormity of philanthropic generosity, of governmental bureaucracy, there are

- the cold
- the old
- the hungry
- the lonely
- the fearful
- the victims
- the casualties
- the rejected
- the crushed
- the alienated

Some of them have managed to avoid the statisticians. We don't always know they're there.

There is still the hope that a revival, bathed in compassion of a genuine biblical rootage rather than syrupy hype, will sweep across and through the body of Christ and rebaptize and renew us.

Is it not natural that the God to whom the tear-catcher would cry would have children anxious to be about the father's business, acting as "Christ's ambassadors, as though God were making his appeal through them" (II Cor. 5:20)?

There are no bands, no parades, no recruitment sales pitches, just an invitation, from him to you. Would you become a tear-catcher in his cadre?

6
RECOGNIZING THOSE WHO CANNOT ASK FOR HELP

Some of them wait in quiet hells
  wondering if we will ever come
Some have been so blinded by their years of tears
  they cannot find the way out.
We must slip to their sides
  and walk with them
  and catch the tears.
For some of the most beautiful sunrises
  are only possible
  because our eyes
  have been cleansed by the tears
  that preceded the dawn.

Tear-catchers must learn early that not everyone can ask for help. Some are too timid; others are afraid that they will be rejected again. Many have been humiliated or "reduced" to tears, and a few have been mercilessly teased. "You big CRYBABY!" has scarred the delicate surface of their soul.

It's easier to respond to those who ask, even if the request comes at an inconvenient time. But it may be more essential to respond to those who do not or cannot ask.

But to be a tear-catcher
    one must really be at home with tears
    not only of those you would touch
but, your own as well.

Their names are unimportant; they are nameless, faceless cogs in our world. Some would term them "the walking wounded." Francis Schaeffer has called our attention to those "humans in an inhuman world."[1]

They have few friends
    fewer neighbors in the real sense of the term
    some acquaintances
They are strangers to concern.

It's so easy to say, "I'm sure everything will work out for you." After all, as evangelicals we're committed to Romans 8:28, right? But how long have they had to tread the floodwaters of their emotional hell? How many so-called friends have turned their backs on them once they knew why they cried?

Has Romans 8:28 lost its freshness and just become another evangelical cliché? Are there not those times in our fervent prayer, "O Lord, help so-and-so, he needs ———," that the Lord taps us on the shoulder and says, "You respond"?

Let's consider those who cannot or do not ask for help.

THE LONE RANGERS

The Lone Ranger at least had Tonto as they swept across the West. Today a host of people

- walk alone
- eat alone
- hurt alone
- die alone

Some come from families which kept a stiff upper lip or kept things to themselves. Such attitudes have caused more chest pain than heart attacks. Others are casualties. Someone disappointed them or abandoned them in a moment of desperation. Many have developed a tradition of being emotionally self-sufficient in this dog-eat-dog world. Besides, if you don't trust anyone, you won't be disappointed (although you might be occasionally surprised).

The Lone Ranger often tracked down an outlaw because of the clues left along the trail. But somehow today it becomes easy to tune out the Maydays of pilgrims desperately calling, "Is anyone there?"

That's why funerals of those who have committed suicide are so bleak. They represent the failure of compassion. No one took the signals seriously.

THE MARTYRS

This group of tear-droppers is populated by those who have tangled with life and come up short. Their anthem is "Life isn't fair!" Well, who said life *had* to be fair? If life were fair,

- Abel would not have died.
- Uriah would not have been killed.
- Job would not have had boils.

But life resists our restrictions.

Their alternate selection is, "They're out to get me!" although the *they* may be somewhat vague.

Real martyrs never know that they are martyrs. The verbal ones who demand that their martyrdom be recognized do not qualify for the fringe benefits. Jesus warned people not to announce they were fasting or the mere recognition of that fact would be their reward. Martyrs can be a little hard to take at times.

It is also possible to carry the torch long after the flame has been extinguished. So many tear-sharers are trying to redo yesterday. We hold on to those who have hurt us and this strokes our vanity and ego.

God can use the defeats in our lives as sandpaper to bring out our grain, *if* we will relinquish the claim checks to self-martyrdom. I remember an autograph party in New Mexico when a woman began crying. She thanked me for my sensitivity in recognizing the needs of middle-aged divorced women. She then proceeded to share the details of her divorce. I finally asked, "How long have you been single—again?"

"Seventeen years," she replied through the tears.

Seventeen years! To keep picking at the scabs of emotional wounds for seventeen years is not the way to grow. Although we tell our children to "leave the scab *alone!*" most adults cannot ignore the mental scabs. So we dance with the pain as we keep looking at our wounds.

We have to let go of our claim checks to yesterday as well.

Frequently, an unwritten rationale for martyrs is "I deserve this," and they usually have a reason. And we come to expect this. Remember Job's three friends who kept wanting him to confess some juicy tidbits of sin in his life?

The tear-catcher cannot always recognize claims of the self-martyr. That intolerance seems uncharacteristic, but it is for the martyr's benefit.

THE HUMILIATED

Because of the source which provoked the tears, some people have assumed part of the stigma themselves. Or else society has insisted on putting the stigma on them. A woman whose husband was arrested for incest soon felt the pressure although she was a victim. People asked, "Where were you while all this was going on?"

Consider the American family who appear to have it all. Then the husband is arrested for soliciting a homosexual act in a public restroom.

Consider the woman who has been accustomed to a good living but discovers her husband is an embezzler.

Some people have the indignity of being stripped of integrity and self-esteem through circumstances over which they had no control. And so they weep.

Sometimes humiliation is silent.

I met a pastor whose wife ran off with a man in the congregation. The deacons quickly met and fired the pastor. With little savings he tried to find a job to put bread on the table. The only work he could find was as a janitor in a large department store.

One morning as he was mopping floors, a member of his congregation came into the store. "Why, Pastor Jones, *what on earth* are you doing mopping floors?" (*How could she not have heard?* he wondered.) He turned and fled into a nearby restroom and wept hysterically for half an hour. "What *am* I doing here, God?" he demanded.

We put ministers on pedestals and woe to them if they or members of their families tumble. We expect ordination to alter all the defects of humanity. Yet some would protest the double standard of expectations.

THE TRAPPED

Perhaps Richard Nixon kept hoping that somehow some morning he would wake up and there would be no more Watergate. Decent people sometimes make stupid decisions because they are trapped; they are exhausted from the pretense and strain. An animal may chew off a leg or foot in order to escape a trap that has ensnared it.

That was the focus of Paul's writing in Galatians, "Brothers, if someone *is caught* in a sin [trapped], you who are spiritual should restore him *gently.*" It's so easy to overlook that adverb. "But watch yourself, or you also may be tempted" (6:1, italics mine).

Sometimes we are the most insensitive on those matters that tempt us. Tear-catchers must always be aware of their own weaknesses.

When I lived in North Carolina, we had a lot of rabbits in our area. Late one night I heard an intense whining that sounded like a child. I went outside and found that something or someone had chased a rabbit. The little fellow had attempted to run through my neighbor's fence, but his back legs were caught by the unbending wire. He couldn't go forward or backward. That rabbit was trapped.

Apparently my arrival on the scene scared away the rabbit's pursuer. I was initially afraid that he would bite me if I attempted to free him from the wire mesh. Finally I held his head to the ground (surely he thought this was selection time for rabbit stew), while with the other hand I pulled the fence apart enough for him to escape me too.

The rabbit never thanked me, but I was able to release him and to prevent his prolonged agony, although it meant some inconvenience on my part. I think I sensed his gratitude as his furry little body scampered into the night.

So it is with the trapped. They may be exhausted from their struggling. By the time they are discovered they may be almost too weak to survive. For others, there is a wave of relief that they no longer have to keep up a pretense. And often they may not say thank you.

That's why "give 'em enough rope and they will hang themselves" is alien to the tear-catcher's repertoire of clichés. It is far too easy to snicker with the woes that infest our brothers and sisters—particularly those we don't like. "You'll get yours!" is always inappropriate.

THE HURT

I once heard Chuck Swindoll tell the story of a child who fell down while playing in the backyard. At that moment the child's mother yelled, "Dinner's ready." She had prepared a nourishing meal and was anxious that everyone eat while everything was hot. She ignored the child's tears and urged, "Eat."

But of course the child couldn't eat. No matter how attractive the food, even if it was the child's favorite, there was a barrier to the child's participation in and enjoyment of the meal. A wise parent would take the time to tend the hurts and then bring the child to the table.

Yet there are thousands of people invited into our fellowships who have been hurt. They need to be bandaged, to be cared for. That's what Paul meant by "carry each other's burdens" (Gal. 6:2).

There is the burden of unheard tears; there are those who weep in isolation. Jesus experienced that loneliness and isolation in order, as Hebrews 2:17 says, "He had to be made like his brothers in every way."

Remember the agony of Gethsemane? Jesus took Peter and James and John with him. He gave verbal and physical signals yet they failed to understand: "My soul is overwhelmed with sorrow"—verbal; "He began to be sorrowful and troubled"—visual; "He fell with his face to the ground"—visual (Matt. 26:37-39).

Yet the trusted disciples slept. Three times he interrupted them. The writer of Hebrews noted that Jesus "offered up prayers and petitions with loud cries and tears to the one who could save him from death" (5:7).

While his disciples slept, "an angel from heaven appeared to him and strengthened him. And being in anguish, he prayed more earnestly, and his sweat was like drops of blood falling to the ground" (Luke 22:43-44).

How odd that his groaning pierced heaven (and he was heard) but not the sleeping of his friends a stone's throw away (Luke 22:41).

So Jesus does understand when we cry, seemingly alone. Had he not experienced the loneliness of Gethsemane, we could not be sure that he understands our Gethsemanes.

There is a tragic irony of humanity in the excuse, "I didn't hear their tears!" The slightest drop of a leaky faucet drives us bananas!

Sometimes it is difficult to resist the temptation to condemn those who have not responded to our tears. Dare we ask, "Why didn't I ask for help?" Jesus did not condemn his three trusted friends. Neither must we. We can rest only in one consolation—that because he has wept alone, he is with us as we weep. Yet there are those times he would nudge us out of our sleep to weep with another.

We can be tear-catchers to those who cannot ask for our help.

7

BARRIERS OR BRIDGES?

My grandfather (and I suppose a lot of other grand-fathers) used to say that you could lead a horse to water but you couldn't make him drink.

Sometimes tear-catchers are in situations where they doubt the commitment of the person to share the tears; some seem to tease the would-be tear-catcher. Jesus said that anyone who came to him had to believe that he was who he said he was. There were many who heard Jesus who went away untouched. We have a peculiar notion that Jesus healed everyone within a two-mile radius.

I have not forgotten one distressed student who came to see me. "I don't know if you can help me or not," he said in what sounded like panic, "but I'm desperate and there's no one to turn to."

"What about our counseling department?" I asked.

"Two weeks to the next vacancy." Then, without pause for a green light from me, he unloaded his bombshell.

My invitation to him to risk that moment, that disclosure, had been a chapel speech on intimacy; one half hour shared with a busy student body. That day, books were closed, conversations abandoned—a response not granted to every chapel speaker. Apparently I had touched the sensitive points of several students.

Although I nourished an ember of hope within that student and others, in doing so I managed to irritate some faculty who thought the subject inappropriate. "Oh, our students wouldn't have *these* kinds of problems." Another group of faculty members would have preferred a discourse on hermeneutical style in obscure passages of Leviticus. But since chapel is required of students, I thought my remarks should be directed to their needs. I've never known college students to weep themselves to sleep struggling with the hermeneutics of Leviticus, but I have known them to toss and turn over intercourse, masturbation, petting, homosexuality, drugs, and other problems.

Actually, if it had not been for that chapel talk, I doubt that I would be writing this book. I had given some thought to the subject of tear-catching, but I was in an academic setting where degrees, credentials, and journal publications were everything. My job was to recruit students and to trust them to the faculty once they were enrolled. Yet somehow that didn't make as much sense to me as it did to the faculty. I had made an investment in some of those students; I had persuaded more than a few to attend.

And there sat one of them. I wondered how long the student had rehearsed his opening lines. How many others, like him, had cursed their cowardice (as much as the problem) as they faced another day with no one to help shoulder the burden? Remember that old song Tennessee Ernie Ford sang, "Sixteen Tons"? I used to sing that on the way to the school bus, "Another day older, and deeper in debt . . ." So it is with those who have unwept tears. They keep hoping things will get better; they covet the miraculous intervention . . . yet it seems to be another day away.

People often come to talk to tear-catchers, disguising their intent until they can see not only "the whites of the eyes" but also the "whites of the soul." So we waltz through the perimeters of surface conversations about sports, the weather, politics, until they make a decision to "spill their guts." Sometimes the problem just flows over the millrace and both sharer and catcher blink.

Others waste time until there are only a few minutes left, and suddenly the problem is "belched" with an excuse-me attitude, "I didn't mean to tell you." One difficulty I had was that I was a member of the administration, associate director of admissions, and that made me suspect with some students. A few thought surely I would pick up the phone and call the dean and say, "Guess what?" But I never did that. I was a lonely administrator, not privy to real decision making, yet alienated from a faculty who thought they had to be cool to administrative staff.

Then there were those students who camouflaged their approach, just in case I broke their confidence and shared with another administrator. "Well, I have this friend, see, and . . . ah, well, he is afraid to come in and talk with you . . . so, ah, well, I thought I would talk to you, and then I could take back to him what you tell me." Did they *really* expect me to believe that? But I sometimes played the game because I remembered those days a decade previously when I played the same game.

Another problem a tear-catcher faces is the time-management syndrome. "I really hate to *bother* you because you're so busy and all . . ." Here the tear-catcher must be on continual guard lest the automatic signals of body english (checking the watch, yawning, failure to maintain eye contact) be interpreted as "You're bothering me!" or "Hurry up!" So we pull out the ancient, rickety cliché, "Oh, you're no bother" or "That's what I am here for," but too often our gestures contradict our proclamation.

Burden-sharers need some immediate reassurance that they have done the right thing in coming to talk to a tear-catcher. The temptation for some is to hit the panic button and make a conversational U-turn (sometimes without a warning signal) and short-circuit the help they need by aborting the conversation. Later they are too often exhausted by the guilt—"I was so close to getting help!"

People getting ready to share a problem expect hurdles or barricades which must be jumped or negotiated. They have experienced these in other conversations, why should this one be different? Besides, that's how most people listen. They erect barricades to slow down the conversation, to give time to think before they select their "prerecorded-for-presentation-in-this-time-zone" responses.

And there are tear-sharers who have practiced before mirrors as intently as any actor before opening night.

WHAT ARE THE BARRIERS?

What are the barriers to be overcome before a person is willing or able to share problems, pains, burdens?

You'll Tell

A tear-catcher must be trustworthy. Some people will be denied this ministry because their name connotes "gossiper" or "leaking sieve." "Whatever you do, don't tell Doris; she tells *everything* she knows," we're cautioned.

Some people can initially be trusted but eventually talk. Remember those old crusty police sergeants in the movies? "Give him to me. I'll make him talk. He'll sing like a bird." Well, all it takes to open some mouths is a promise, "I won't tell a soul," whether or not we really mean it.

Some tear-sharers have so nourished their self-contempt that they assume everyone from district attorney to sheriff is interested in their confession. These are the sort of folk who, amazingly, after media disclosure of sensational murders, often turn themselves in and confess to the crime, although they have no tie whatever to the case. The need for confession is acute in our society.

Sometimes tear-catchers respond to a person's fear by saying, "Wild horses couldn't drag it out of me. My lips are sealed!" But many of us realize how little it takes to loosen most tongues. So we need to reassure the tear-sharer.

That's what is so reassuring about the "sea of God's forgetfulness." Jesus has never told *anyone* about a single sin that we have confessed. His lips are sealed.

If only more of his children would emulate him!

I'm Afraid to Trust

We've all known those moments of betrayal when someone squealed or when our confession became public domain. That's what makes Hollywood magazines such a business—people want to know the dirt on the stars. We love to gossip about other people's failures.

Someone whose confidence has been betrayed may threaten, "I'll get you for this," but most of them scurry for a barrier behind which to hide until they can assess the damage. And they keep frantically searching for someone else who can be trusted. One reason for buying counseling time is that we also buy confidentiality.

A person with a desperate need to share also tends to toy with the paranoia alarm. The inner tapes play and replay their accusations: "You're a fraud!" "If they only knew what you were *really* like!" "What if they knew about . . ." Those accusations wound and maim and keep many from the fountains of healing.

Sidney Jourard noted this fear in *The Transparent Self.* Authentic sharing is risky.

> The chief risk lies in letting other people know how one has experienced the events impinging on one's life. All that other people can ever see of an individual is the expurgated version he discloses through his action. A man's public utterances are often radically different from what he authentically feels and believes. *Many of us dread to be known by others as intimately as we know ourselves because we would be divorced, fired or shot.*[1]

And some tear-sharers would add, "or all three!"

Because of my area of ministry, when I speak, I change cities, dates, and sexes to protect individuals. "Then why tell the story at all?" you might ask. Only because life-scripts are not that unusual; we all share experiences. "No temptation has seized you except what is common to man. And God is faithful; he will not let you be tempted beyond what you can bear. But when you are tempted, he will also provide a way out so that you can stand up under it," we are told (I Cor. 10:13).

That "way out" may be the testimony of a brother or sister. Indeed, that is the reason for some people's fall—our failure to stand beside them in their temptation. Bonhoeffer wrote, "The basis upon which Christians can speak to one another is that each knows the other is a sinner, who, with all his human dignity, is lonely and lost if he is not given help."[2]

Again, Paul's statement comes to mind, that we can comfort one another "with the comfort we ourselves have received from God" (II Cor. 1:4). Many problems of tear-sharers could be lessened (as would be the scars) if we were more prompt.

Jerry Hull shared an incredible thought in an article on homosexuality published in *One* magazine. "The plight of 52 hostages imprisoned by the desperate hatred of frustrated terrorists led most of us to urgent prayers. What of the millions held in bondage by much greater captors?"[3]

The most vulnerable, needy people are often afraid to trust. Remember the woman who came to Jesus "having spent all" on physicians and still ill? What made her trust him?

When I moved to Kansas City, a friend gave me a present. "If you ever need to talk to someone, call ————," and he gave me a name. "He'll never repeat a word." That has been like money in the bank for a rainy day—someone I can trust. Texaco used to advertise, "You can trust your car to the man who wears the star. The big, bright, Texaco star." Well, to whom do we trust our scar? or the scab that will become the scar?

I wish tear-catchers were easier to spot in a crowd.

This Confession Makes Me Vulnerable

"Since I have told you, what will you think of me *now*?" Friendships are so fragile, so shallow. We're afraid to risk! Could you use what I have told you against me in a moment of anger? or for a little polite extortion? or to tease?

I have a friend who leads seminars on trust and friendship. He takes participants through a series of questions:

- How many of you have a good friend?
- How many of you have a friend that would stick with you no matter what?
- How many of you would loan money to this friend?

- How many of you could call this friend and borrow money?
- Would this friend post your bond if you were arrested on a child-molesting charge?

Generally the room goes quiet with that last question. Friendships are shallow and convenient.

This fear of vulnerability has kept many tear-sharers from the altar of confession or from counseling. The fear is nourished by two childhood tapes.

1. "I love you, but I don't have to like you. Children are taught in Sunday school that they *have* to love everyone, but some way they get the notion that it's OK not to like some people. So we say to a gay person, "I have to love you in the Lord, but I'm not going to shake your hand or invite you to my home for dinner."

An interesting thing happened during a revival in a church that has an altar where people come to make religious commitments. A man had come several nights, carefully listening, observing. He noticed how people gathered around to pray with "the seekers." One night a man with a notorious reputation went forward on the invitation, and again the people gathered to pray.

When he stood up, people hugged him or shook his hand and told him they were praying for him. The young observer thought, "Behold, how they love one another. There must be something authentic about these people."

The next night, after the evangelist's sermon, he went forward. The people gathered to pray, and one man suggested, "If we confess our sins, he is faithful and just to forgive us." So the young man confessed and the altar area became deathly hushed. He was a homosexual.

The prayer was polite. After a few moments, all stood. But this time there were no handshakes, no hugs, just an embarrassed silence.

We do believe in a ranking system of sin, don't we? Oh, it's not in our creeds or our liturgies or our publications, but it is in our hearts. The evangelical version of the Pharisees! Yet that was not a problem for Paul, who wrote "that is what some of you were" (I Cor. 6:11). Confession is a scary experience, and some have been caught in a vise: the attack of their enemy and the silence of the body of believers.

We talk so much about "hating the sin, loving the sinner" that sometimes a reasonable doubt of the accuracy of the statement remains in the sinner's mind.

2. Did your parents ever demand, "Aren't you ashamed of yourself?" That was "begging the question" in logic, as I recall. But my mother went a step further and asked, "What if Mrs. ———," my current Sunday school teacher, "heard about this? What would she say?" That tape terrorized my spirit the way a band of desperadoes terrorized frontier towns in TV westerns. Most of the time I didn't want Mrs. ——— to know; I was spending too much energy trying to get her to like me.

So we spend our time not building bridges to improve communication but spreading tacks in the road to slow down the sleuth on our trail. We want to cover our tracks, and sometimes we're exhausted from all the effort it takes to do that. How many philanthropists have acted on the assumption that enough good deeds would balance the scales or deflect public opinion if their true selves should be discovered.

We are no more comfortable with nakedness (physical or emotional) than were Adam and Eve. We still want to hide. And some of our disguises are as foolish and inadequate as were Adam's and Eve's.

It Will Obligate Me to Accept Your Advice

A lot of people shop around for bargains in confronting problems or making decisions. Some are like veteran garage-sale enthusiasts or sales seekers who cannot enjoy an item unless they got it on sale.

All tear-catchers have dealt at some time with the transient tear-sharers. Some resemble the rich young ruler who sadly turned away from Jesus because of the high cost of discipleship.

Some want counseling or tear-catching without cost or accountability. Others want to ration the tears or limit the sharing to surface problems rather than facing the real irritants. So many demand instant and painless solutions.

What happens if I share my tears with you and then, after talking over coffee with Helen, I decide I like her advice better? So it's easier not to get involved. Besides, who knows, in a few days the whole thing will blow over anyway. Nothing to get excited about!

I'll Tell You in Small Dosages

This motivation is like an iceberg; whatever we see, as tear-catchers we must remember that 90 percent is hidden under the surface. Or it may more accurately resemble a jigsaw puzzle—sometimes the tear-sharer wants us to assemble the pieces without having seen the picture on the box to know what the puzzle will look like when completed. Sometimes the missing piece is withheld because, if revealed, it would implicate another person.

Some tear-sharers only want the pressure reduced. That way there's more storage space for expansion. Some people approach God's forgiveness in the same thought-stream. They think he periodically forgives to clear out the old sins to make room for tomorrow's.

Many problems are like cancer. You can operate—but unless you get all of it, it will grow back. But the tear-catcher must ask, like the surgeon, "How much good tissue do you remove to make certain you have all the bad?"

Another aspect of this approach is that it is somewhat protective. If I find you have violated my confidence, at least you don't know all the story.

Let's Talk About It Later

These tear-sharers agree to talk "sometime" but definitely "not now." Time complicates the burden; some solutions are eliminated. Many want the optimum setting for disclosure. Yet procrastination is a nutrient that encourages the problem to multiply and at the same time tightens its tentacles around our spirits.

A lot of people die from cancer needlessly because they delayed seeking medical attention.

You'll Say, "I Told You So!"

Four words, ten letters comprise the largest barrier to mental health and spiritual growth. Those words, *I told you so*, cripple vulnerable people. It's like someone complicating our wounds or injuries.

We do have to discriminate in sharing tears, just as we do in getting help with electrical outages, or car problems. For example, I cannot be consulted on car repairs. Under the hood of a car (sometimes behind the wheel), I'm illiterate. So I don't even try to repair my own car. I consult good mechanics.

Some people, particularly the soap-box psychologists, are proud of their track records—their successes. Some are so sure of the "inspiredness" of their advice. Incidentally, that's why there are so many how-to psychology books in the bookstores. Readers know no one has a corner on the market. So they purchase the latest book which makes them feel better that they didn't take the advice of the previous best seller they bought. Some people create small how-to libraries in their homes; they never get around to implementing that advice, but they're always ready to pass it on.

Some pop psychologists are insecure; others are affected by the "messiah" complex, "I have to rescue people." So when their advice is rejected or not followed, they retort, "I told you so"—or worse, they *demand*, "Didn't I tell you so?"

"*If* you had only listened to me, you wouldn't be in this mess, would you?"

"I tried to tell you, but you wouldn't listen!"

A few self-deprecate their own advice. "I tried to tell you, but what would I know about it? I am *only* a salesman," or a taxi driver or a teacher.

Who wouldn't want to be recognized as a son or daughter of Solomon for their wisdom? But seizing the title generally means that rejection bruises the ego. Naturally they retort, "How dare you not take my advice!"

Our world is used to free advice. When we consider how many amateur psychologists, amateur lawyers, and amateur surgeons are on the loose, it is no wonder we have problems. And some of those dispense their opinions without invitation. They merely back up their mental sixteen-wheeler and hit the "dump" button. The next thing we know we're clawing our way through tons of verbiage and advice.

Remember: in the "I told you so's" the emphasis is always on "I." So when you see one coming, go ahead and steal the thunder, and respond, "I know what you're going to say, 'I told you so.' "

Authentic tear-catchers ignore the temptation to announce, "I told you so!" and are *not* offended *when* their advice is rejected. They follow the Master's example. Remember how he warned Peter that he would deny him three times—yet Peter scoffed? Conspicuously absent in the biblical record is any encounter after the Resurrection in which Jesus reminded Peter, "I told you so!"

The impact of those words cannot be diffused. "I told you so" is the shrapnel of human communication that infects the wounded, those least able to fight off complications.

OVERCOMING THE BARRIERS

A tear-catcher dreads barriers like a ship captain fears the rocky, shallow coast which can rip the bottom from his ship. As lighthouses illumine the shores, so we need people to shine, to assist us as we navigate troubled waters.

Tear-catching and tear-sharing are commitments of trust. Sometimes the trust is like a small but glowing ember; it must be carefully nurtured to ignite the fire that will bring warmth and light.

So a tear-catcher is continually seeking to reduce barriers. Occasionally, previous differences must be resolved. A tear-catcher does not hesitate to confess, "I'm sorry" or "I was wrong" or to ask, "Will you forgive me?" These ten words, if made part of our everyday vocabulary, could radically change the world. A tear-catcher realizes that one can be technically correct or accurate and still be wrong because of attitude. It's too tempting to insert elipses after the words *I was wrong* and launch an expedition: "BUT SO WERE YOU. AND YOU WERE MORE WRONG THAN I WAS!"

I may be the tear-catcher most equipped or most readily available to help you. But if my service is hamstrung because of unfinished personal clashes or negative previous encounters, my skills and my competence mean little.

The task for a tear-catcher is to turn barriers into bridges. I remember as a small boy watching the construction of the Sherman Minton Bridge linking Louisville, Kentucky, and New Albany, Indiana. I longed for a new bridge because the old K & I Railroad Bridge frightened me every time we crossed.

But the new bridge was not built overnight.

Why then do we insist that relationships be built instantaneously? Perhaps because we are such an instant people: we want our TV sets to come on immediately; we want the light to change "now" or the car to start on the first turn of the key; we're committed to instant tea and coffee, so why not instant relationships?

The tear-catcher waits, patiently. And because of that patience, a tear-catcher can make a difference!

8

QUALIFICATIONS OF A TEAR-CATCHER

What does it mean to be a tear-catcher? Why would one want to become involved in such a demanding, draining enterprise?

The Lord does not call us to a ministry of frustration, but rather to one of obedience. There are as many motives as there are volunteers, and who but the Lord really knows the heart?

But let's examine the qualifications.

A TEAR-CATCHER KNOWS WHO HE OR SHE IS

Tear-catchers must have confidence in their relationship with God, their sonship or daughtership.

Tear-catchers are sure of their eternal citizenship not as a source of prideful arrogance but of continual hope.

Tear-catchers know who they are because they know *whose* they are. There is a sense of acceptance, of chosenness that warms the tear-catcher on the longest, coldest night.

This is what the Lord says—
". . . Fear not, for I have redeemed you;
I have summoned you by name; you are mine.

When you pass through the waters,
   I will be with you;
and when you pass through the rivers,
   they will not sweep over you.
When you walk through the fire,
   you will not be burned." (Isa. 43:1, 2)

What a promise! That text seems to be God's promise that he will catch my tears.

Henri Nouwen remarked that our society "is much more inclined to help a person hide his pain than to grow through it." So it requires "a conscious effort to mourn."[1] Yet an essential element of God's commitment to us is that he stands with us in our mourning.

There will be times when tear-catchers must reaffirm their calling. Jesus continually pulled away from the crowds and occasionally from the disciples to commune with his Father. How much more do we need such times of renewal if we are to survive the thick fogs of our society! Yet there are those who pride themselves on their warranted spiritual batteries that will start in any condition and never need recharging. Unfortunately spiritual batteries do run down when they aren't recharged.

A TEAR-CATCHER BALANCES THE REALITIES OF THIS WORLD WITH THOSE OF THE NEXT

Remember the old classic, "Oh Think of the Home over There"? Somehow we're fascinated by the streets of gold and uncomplex, unclouded days.

Children learn early about Santa Claus, the Easter Bunny, the Tooth Fairy, as well as the Boogie Man. These serve to explain, at least partially, the unexplainable until the child has enough maturity to understand the existence of that which cannot be explained. Fantasy is a way of incorporating the portions of reality we can understand into the overall picture.

Have you ever worked a jigsaw puzzle and been stuck on a particular piece that almost fits? I recall working on one puzzle with a partner, and I was anxious to move on to something more exciting. So I pointed out something across the room, and while his attention was diverted I got the reluctant piece to fit—well, somewhat.

Occasionally in life we are tempted to force the pieces of the puzzle into place.

There are many Christian workers who are so attuned to the other world that they are of no earthly good. That's why I have some discomfort with prophecy fans. It's both titillating and frightening and yet warming to know that the evil people are going to get "what's coming to them," that is, what we assume should be coming to them. But too many have given up on this world and are resisting planting the seeds of hope in a hostile soil. The temptation, the desire to flee or escape must be controlled.

The reality is that John 3:16 can be paraphrased to read, "For God so loved *this* world, that he gave his only begotten son . . ." (author's interpretation). So how can we despise a world he loves and seeks to redeem?

This is the world he would have us bring under his lordship.

Unfortunately, there is no shortage of hand-wringers standing on the sidelines saying, "What are we gonna do? What are we gonna do?" Maybe we need a moratorium on singing, "This world is not my home," and instead learn to sing, "This *is* my Father's world."

I think God wonders when his church is going to grow up. Must the church forever struggle in its adolescence?

I believe God longs for a generation of tear-catchers who would "march into hell for a heavenly cause."

The greatest threat to mankind is
a generation without tears!
A generation who looks the other way
as tears fall.

A TEAR-CATCHER HAS EXPERIENCED
BROKENNESS AND FORGIVENESS

The tear-catcher has experienced both sides of life: the depths and the heights.

In that unmerited forgiveness he has received, he assumes a debt that can only be repaid in service to others. But because he has been there, he is anxious that others not be there alone.

I have a friend, my age, whose ministry has been placed on the bunsen burner of life. He has made three trips to the cemetery in the last two years: a father, a son, and most recently a wife. He pastors a church and yet tries to be father *and* mother to his children.

Somehow I believe he will find a deeper ministry than some of his colleagues. This time in his life tests the quality of his life. I believe he will be found worthy.

Paul wrote the Corinthians, "Praise be to the God and Father of our Lord Jesus Christ . . . the God of all comfort who comforts us in all our troubles" (II Cor. 1:3-4). We're so excited about that promise that we erect a stop sign. We pause to enjoy the promise. But the Apostle did not stop there in that sentence. God does not comfort us to get us to "shut up." Rather, he "comforts us in all our troubles, so that we can comfort those in any trouble with the comfort we ourselves have received" (verse 4).

His comfort, however affirming and encouraging, makes us debtors. Sometimes it is through the testing fire that we emerge with the smell of smoke that others can immediately sense.

God does not ask our permission or request that we sign release forms. Rather, he stands with us.

A TEAR-CATCHER AVOIDS RELIGIOUS JARGON

Language never remains the same. Look at the words of the eighties which were nonexistent in the early seventies. But there are those who seek to minister through "stained-glass" voices or in the English of King James. The tear-catcher knows the language of the real world as well as the language of eternity.

We overwork the clichés we have heard. I had a pastor friend who called on a new convert to pray in the evening service. The convert strung together a group of prayer clichés and prayed, "Oh Lord, you know about our falling shorts," to which my friend responded, "Pull them up!"

It is too easy to rely on the trite, the memorized, the chichés which may have had significance a generation ago but have become worn out. We have a tendency to stockpile them for instant recall when we don't quite know what to say.

Sometimes, according to the Quakers, the Lord accepts our silence. A handshake, a tear, a hand on the shoulder, a squeeze, can speak more eloquently, more effectively than a flowery monologue. There is the ministry of presence—just being there.

The other day a young man came up after a seminar and confessed that he was "warring with the flesh" and other King Jamesesque statements. Finally I asked, "Are you trying to tell me you're *horny*?"

The type of language he used turned off many who could have helped him as well as those he could have helped.

A TEAR-CATCHER REFRESHES OTHERS

Have you ever been cared for, far beyond the essentials—almost babied or pampered? That's one reason I enjoy the Christmas season. My mother delights in cooking and baking the favorites of each family member. It is important that the oldest and the youngest members of the family find she has remembered them. So it's jam cake for a sister, red velvet cake for a nephew, German chocolate for another, and a saltless recipe for one family member who is on a restricted diet.

And when company comes, they have their choice. She is a gracious hostess; she refreshes others.

Remember Judas' questions about the appropriateness of the woman's costly anointment of Jesus; that it could have been sold and the money given to the poor? Yet Jesus had a need, and the woman sensed it and responded.

The heat in Kansas City during the summer is worse than a dragon's breath. You're "beat" by two o'clock. All you want is to go somewhere and try to keep cool. You envision a cold, beaded glass of iced tea or a bowl of orange sherbet. But it's not as much fun when you have to fix it yourself. The greatest refreshment is to receive a cool drink from a friend. It is not by accident that the Word speaks of hospitality. After all, the One we serve had no place to lay his head. He spent his last week in the home of friends in Bethany.

Paul wrote, "Share with God's people who are in need. Practice hospitality" (Rom. 12:13). One way to refresh others is by putting them at ease. Some people need to be made comfortable enough to share. That's why the design of a pastor's or counselor's office is so crucial. Some environments are more conducive to conversation and confession.

Many tear-catchers have a way of making kitchens or patios or dens feel warm; a person immediately feels at home. I have sat around many kitchen tables and talked about some of the most important things in the world.

My parents have a rather small home without a den or dining room or even a second bath. I often coveted those friends' homes who had all the extra room. But in our home the kitchen was always warm. The kitchen table was the center of activity: I've iced cookies there, written term papers, wrapped surprises, and more than once laid my head down for a nap.

When I was in college and went home for a weekend, no matter what time I arrived, Mom would ask, "Are you hungry?" Then we sat around the table and talked.

Tear-catchers must refresh others. Many sessions of tear-sharing have taken place over coffee or tea. Sometimes, just the suggestion, "Let's go get a cup of coffee" is a message. My colleague at Point Loma College, Dr. Cecil Miller, rounded up a group of administrators at 9:30 every work day for what he called "therapy."

What appears to an outsider to be casual chatter is often a nucleus of building blocks. Sometimes, ideas are tested over coffee. "Well, if he's open on that subject," a person thinks, "he *might* be open to the topic I really want to discuss." Coffee breaks prime the pump. Sometimes, though, the timing doesn't seem quite right or the person waits until too late and someone notices the clock. Often, however, in those times of refreshment, we open the door through which they will later walk to shed their tears.

A TEAR-CATCHER WAITS . . . PATIENTLY

We're a generation of clock- or watch-watchers; we know the subtle ways to turn our wrist to discover the time without seeming bored or impatient.

Yet we are impatient. We allow a few moments of conversational warmup, but we want to get to the point. This preliminary chatter gives us a chance to gauge the mood of the listener. Some people immediately ask, "What's on your mind?" to bring the preliminaries to a close. A few have learned to be a bit more diplomatic: "How can I help you?"

I am impatient but am working on the problem. I've become impatient with learning to be patient! There have been those times I've waited and waited for some people to get to the point. And at times, I have communicated my impatience too effectively and have wounded a tear-sharer.

People are so used to the cliché, "I hate to bother you . . ." while expecting and discounting the response, "Oh, you're no bother," that they spend a lot of time making sure this is the best time to come with their problems. But being "bothered" is an appeal to the ego—"I am so important," or "I have such important work to do." That attitude leads to pride. Bonhoeffer contended that the Lord is anxious to interrupt us.

But it's tough to wait. What happens if thirty seconds of silence follow a commercial on TV? We get impatient, edgy. Some of us even speak to the TV: "Well, come on," and a few have been known to give it a friendly tap. Sports commentators seek to occupy every second of air time with fillers or trivia or mere verbiage—meaningless words.

But tear-catchers wait. They may be aware of the *why* behind the tears but want the tear-sharers to disclose the information on their own schedule. In many cases people have a carefully rehearsed script (or alternate scripts) to explain. A few have even role-played their responses.

Sometimes a tear-sharer has learned that once a listener starts to respond, the speaker has lost control of the conversation. How often does a tear-sharer have to insert, "Let me finish" or "Hear me out before you say anything"?

Of course we reply, "Oh, I let them talk," but often while listening we are mentally pretesting our own responses rather than fully listening. That's why we so frequently misunderstand even the simplest communication.

Some must, of course, maintain the tradition of brilliance which has earned them labels: "He *always* knows what to do; why don't you talk to him?" However, the reputation as a "know-what-to-doer" or a "loophole discoverer" or an "escape clausist" can be a barrier to sensitive ministry. It's too easy to begin forming our responses before the speaker has taken a good breath. As a writer, I edit my drafts before I submit them to an editor. Some listeners work the same way: scratching out words, pretesting conclusions, italicizing sentences even while the other person is still speaking.

It's embarrassing to say, "I don't know what to say," and thereby perhaps cause the tear-sharer further pain. But even if the person has to demand, "Well, don't just sit there. Say something!" that is better than our saying the wrong thing. By becoming impatient we can confront the person prematurely.

One friend who prides himself on his counseling skills has a repertoire which includes

- "Isn't this *really* your problem . . . ?"
- "You know what's wrong with you . . ."
- "Your *real* problem is . . ."
- "It seems to me that . . ."
- "Why don't you admit it . . . ?"

No one is going to waste his time beating around the bush! He believes in ambushing people who come to him: he confronts. He claims this technique saves a lot of time. When he senses someone is wasting his time, he cuts through the fog to get to the heart of the matter. Besides, he has a string of informants and a belief in hunch. On more than one occasion he has forced people into premature confessions.

Yet he finds tear-catching ineffective.

God always condemns the pride of ego that causes us to overvalue the worth of our time. Although we do need to be wise stewards of our time, we must allow for those who are shy, who struggle with words, or who want to put the best foot forward so they will appear in the best possible light.

One test of tear-catching (and friendship) is the luxury of silence. To be able to share silence rather than use or manipulate others through a technique is a rare art form in today's world. Too many of us struggle to keep conversations going by putting twigs on the fire rather than great logs.

That's what I especially enjoy—those friends with whom I can get together and be silent.

But there are times when the tear-catcher gives distance. A "give me a call if you want to talk" says "I'm available." A tear-catcher can say, "Do you want to talk about *it?*" as an invitation rather than a command.

As tear-sharers, however, we must not become impatient if others do not recognize the double meanings of our silence. Many couples struggle through their silence. Finally, one mate asks, "What's wrong?"

"Wrong?" (*discounts*) "What makes you think something is wrong?"

"Well, you're pretty quiet."

"I'm tired."

"Are you sure nothing's wrong?"

"Well, if you don't know, I'm not going to tell you!"

or

"I don't want to talk about it!"

Then patience snaps. "Well, we're going to talk about it. Now!"

The tear-catcher waits.

A TEAR-CATCHER IS SENSITIVE
TO THOSE WHO WEEP

A tear-catcher recognizes tears as a treasured gift. There
is a legend
>   of an old man
>   who walked alone
>   on a frigid night
>   with no one to catch his tears.
>   So, along the familiar path
>   he shed his tears.
>   The next morning
>   he arose early
>   and as he walked
>   that familiar path
>   He found it strewn with diamonds.

A tear-catcher doesn't merely "kiss it to make it go
away." Sometimes the problem will not go away, there
are no simplistic solutions, and it becomes a permanent
resident of the soul. But there can be fresh perspectives.

The tear-catcher recognizes the importance of crying
as a lubricant for the conversation that follows the tears.
Sometimes tears sanitize the passageways from the spirit
to the listener—to insure the survival of the tears.

Some of us have been ashamed of our tears; we have
chosen the quiet, lonely places to shed them. Jesus
encountered a demon-possessed man who "lived in the
tombs." Mark reports, "Night and day among the tombs
and in the hills he would cry out and cut himself with
stones" (Mark 5:5).

When Jesus encountered him, he could not leave him in
the tombs. Nor can we leave those we find in the dark
places. Archie Bunker's line, "Stifle!" somehow taunts. It
is not a line for a tear-catchers. "Quit crying" or "Don't

cry" must become invitations rather than demands. In some cases, such a response only produces more tears.

We've aborted too many tears—tears that could have formed an oasis for the next pilgrim on that trail.

We've condemned our own tears and thus denied our God-given design. We've sinned against ourselves and we've passed that from generation to generation; thus the healing has been denied.

A tear-catcher does not squirm or twist nervously when another cries. A tear-catcher is comfortable with tears—he finds them neither repulsive nor contaminating.

A tear-catcher recognizes that God has designed and equipped us to cry; a tear-catcher gives permission.

Tear-phobia has paralyzed many who would catch tears. An army which cannot weep cannot rejoice. The movie *Patton* contains a scene in which George Patton slaps a weeping soldier while visiting a military hospital. General Eisenhower demanded that the general apologize to the private. And he did.

Eisenhower recognized the appropriateness of tears and won a spot in the hearts of the American people.

> We are designed to cry
>   and to respond to another's tears.
> As a result
>   we are never more God's design
>   than when we cry
> And never more the redeemed
>   than when we catch another's tears.

A tear-catcher simply catches tears without intimidating the one who shed the tears or questioning what initiated the tears.

9

DISCIPLINES OF A TEAR-CATCHER

A tear-catcher must be disciplined. "Many are called, but few are chosen" were the words Jesus used to describe his followers (Matt. 22:14 RSV). The same is true for tear-catchers.

We live in a day of easy membership, of watered-down standards, of defective craftsmanship. It is so easy to hear an inspirational speaker or read an inspirational book, and respond by saying, "I'd like to do that," but then do nothing at all—never put what we know into practice.

Ann Kiemel, in *I'm Running to Win*, recounts the blood, sweat, and tears of running the Boston Marathon, 26.3 miles. Many people have read her book and heard her speak, but how many have gone out to train for their own entry into a race?

What are the disciplines that produce a tear-catcher?

A TEAR-CATCHER DISCIPLINES TIME

It takes time to be a tear-catcher. Time to become, time to be, time to listen, time to wait. We live in a busy, hurry-hurry, on-the-go generation. I cannot forget Rodney Dangerfield's great one-liner. Someone tried to stop him to talk, but Dangerfield replied, "Don't have time to talk."

"Why?" asked the friend.

"Someone told me to go jump in the lake, and I'm late."

Look at the following cliché: "I'd like to help, but ———" and you merely fill in the blank. We stockpile a repertoire of ready-made excuses. Suppose a good friend is moving to a new apartment next weekend. You respond, "Wouldn't you know it would be this weekend? I'd like to help, but ———."

We're a time-conscious people. Businesses spend a great deal of money on time-management studies in order to economize time. After all, "Time is money!" As a result of such a study, I was hired to make ice water every day. The firm for which I worked had forty men making eight dollars per hour. Each morning they *each* took an hour to make ice water (due to a union regulation, each truck had to have a jug of ice water on it). Each day the company was spending $320 on ice water. Finally, a management specialist had them hire me for the minimum wage.

Notice the time-saving appliances we give a new couple as they set up housekeeping. Walk through your kitchen and inventory all the items that your grandmother never had: steam iron, blender, microwave oven, dishwasher, mixer, electric knife. We defend the purchase because "it saves so much time."

Consider the tremendous development in processed foods.

One only has to look at the amount of energy required to run these appliances and make the processed foods to understand some of the reasons for the energy crisis. Grandmothers and great-grandmothers used muscle-power or child-power.

Somehow, despite perma-press and microwave technology, we're still pressed for time. So many things just don't get done or properly done. We look in astonishment at the working mother, especially the working single parent, who somehow manages to get it all done.

Some busy people juggle schedules like bouncing balls; they must be attuned to an intricate schedule; a few become captives. And we have developed a slogan, "Want something done—give it to a busy person." We have not escaped the Puritan notion, "Idle hands are the devil's workshop."

Many people who would like to help are hindered by their inability to prioritize their time—to make room for tear-catching. Yet some tear-catchers go overboard and leave no time for recharging their own batteries.

The church is led by a regiment of workaholics. John Claypool maintains the church is being led by "tired" men. Senior pastors routinely put in eighty-hour work weeks; even young leaders are under such work loads that fatigue is expected and normal. Yet "burnout" articles are appearing more frequently in journals. Why do we work so hard?

Americans are afraid of loneliness and aloneness. Many people deny that loneliness is part of the human condition. We hear about "the poor, lonely, single adults." Well, I've been married and single—and have been lonely in both states. Loneliness *is* part of the human condition.

We may try to insulate ourselves from the reality of loneliness. By packing so many events into our day, we hope to fall into bed exhausted and thus avoid the aloneness that teases in those moments before sleep.

Americans are also afraid of silence; we have moved radios, stereos, and televisions into our bedrooms. Some adults resemble the child who cannot go to sleep without the night lamp. Only our nightlights are audio. Some of us reach for the newspaper and coffee while still half-asleep.

"I'd like to help" or "I'd *really* like to help" (don't forget to add "maybe next time") are common clichés. Some people, however, have designed a counter-strategy: *guilting*. Skillfully, they can produce a fog of guilt: "You should help me!"

Consider a little child who wants an adult to play with him. Why, doesn't he know how busy adults are? When the child asks for the fifteenth time and the adult says, "Can't you see I'm busy?" through gritted teeth, his little expression is heartbreaking. Through guilt the adult responds, "OK, but just for a few minutes, OK?" So the child begins learning the process of manipulating people through massaging pseudoguilt.

How many people spend time with aging parents out of a sense of guilt: "After all I've done for you," or "Mrs. Jones's daughters come to see her, why don't you come to see me?" Yet it is demeaning to visit from a sense of obligation rather than desire or interest.

And the church has perfected the guilting strategy. "If you were the kind of Christian you ought to be, you'd volunteer to teach that Sunday school class . . . or you'd participate in the Bible study or . . ." and the list is endless.

Before accepting another time demand, we need to consider that some people spiritualize loneliness by planning yet another religious activity. Some churches have something scheduled every night of the week and all day on Sunday . . . hardly the day of rest!

Too often we have collectively filled our schedules (and because of age segmentation programming in most churches, there are overlaps and conflicts). We've allowed lonely people to provide the role models and guilt-stroke us into compliances.

Finally, some Christians must courageously say, "Enough!" A tear-catcher must discipline time and prioritize the demands to make time for people rather than programs.

When I first started doing single-adult seminars, I accepted every invitation to speak. As a result, my time for writing was severely curtailed. Eventually I discovered that I could not be at my best when I assumed invitations that fatigued me. The result was my cisterns ran dry. Have you ever explained to a child who wanted a soda that there wasn't any soda? or that the machine was out of order?

Tear-catchers must carefully examine the commitment to give away their time.

- Am I seeking to escape problems at home?
- Am I seeking my halo prematurely?
- Am I avoiding confrontation/conflict in my own life?

Some people have been so busy saving everyone else's children that they have lost their own children: a tragedy of the first order. That is why Paul suggested that an overseer "must manage his own family well" (I Tim. 3:4).

A TEAR-CATCHER DISCIPLINES RISK

The second element that influences a tear-catcher is risk.

As we have reduced our global military responsibility, we have redefined the parameters of humanity. What does it mean to be human and a neighbor? So what if some dictator somewhere squelches human rights. That's no sweat off my back! Isn't it?

Once this redefining the territory gets started, it's difficult to limit it to political considerations. My definition of the label *neighbor* is quite different from that held by my grandfathers who were farmers in Indiana. Then a neighbor's harvest was as important as theirs; if a barn needed repairing, the community pitched in. These values were often inculturated through the community one-room school.

In the Age of the Me, we ask, "What's in it for me?" After a decade of noninvolvement, is it so difficult to understand why no one defends a woman from a purse-snatcher or mugger or rapist—unless it is *your* mother or *your* daughter or *your* wife.

"Don't get involved" or "It's not your fight" have become engraved on our consciousness. As a result of such thinking, we decide where we will expend our energy and ammunition.

In our jobs we've watched colleagues be harrassed or fired. Sometimes we have acquiesced in cowardice and been conveniently "gone" as they cleaned out their desks. We may be able to commiserate over coffee about their "getting the shaft" and yet feel no responsibility to challenge the shafter. "That's the way it is!"

We've become afraid to defend others' rights lest the aggressors turn on us. That fear has inevitably infiltrated the church; we do not easily negate our Monday through Friday world's impact on the church house.

In our success-oriented society, risk has become so calculated as to demean the word. Tax laws take the burden and blessing out of risk. The adrenaline is seldom as high as in risk situations.

We use the slang, "Go for it," but you'd better count the cost. I have a friend whose marriage died because of an oil well. He had had a chance to buy in on "a sure thing." However, his wife banked everything at 6 percent or bought U.S. savings bonds and talked him out of the investment because of the risk.

The well was a gusher!

Dreams are fueled on planned or calculated risk.

Some tear–catchers have resigned their ordination because of risk's toll. In a moment of fatigue or disappointment they murmured, "Never again!"

What are the risks of being a tear-catcher?

Those who catch tears always risk being misunderstood. Someone will always question your motives. Count on it. We've watched so many soap operas and R-rated movies that we routinely suspect a sexual motivation in every male-female interchange.

Admittedly, some tear-catchers have been shelved because of indiscriminate behavior. But an equal number have been side-tracked by the paranoid fantasies of noninvolved people. This reality led Origen, a tear-catcher of the third century, to castrate himself and thus put himself above suspicion, although few have followed his dramatic but effective example.

Those who catch tears must risk having their advice or wisdom rejected (or replaced by a discount brand). There is the trace of Solomon's ego in all of us; we want to be known for our wisdom. We spend a lot of time dispensing it, and then, if it is rejected, we may conclude, "Why bother?" (And we often punctuate it with an exclamation point rather than the question mark.)

We bother because a safeless, riskless life is anemic.

Those who catch tears risk accommodation. A recent magazine article carried information on police undercover agents who assume certain identities to infiltrate crime settings. These agents are monitored closely because they tend to accommodate to certain characteristics of the group.

Unquestionably, this factor necessitates occasional time-outs for the tear-catcher to avoid burnout.

Those who catch tears risk becoming experts or being quoted out of context. The tear-sharer may quote you out of context and the new hearer may repeat or edit your words without the qualifiers you used. Eventually, the public view may differ radically from the original statement. People hear what they want to hear. Some merely go through the process hoping you will confirm what they have already concluded or applaud the decision they have made.

The temptation for many tear-catchers is to want to be accepted or become a best seller whose fame goes before them. To become expert or an authority so that your views or opinions weigh greater than X's can be costly.

We cannot forget that Saul stood head and shoulders above all the people (I Sam. 10:23), and yet he failed.

I am not an expert—just another pilgrim willing to share information about my experience with the trail. I wish things were black OR white—but the Torah's 630 rules (and easy one-two-three answers memorized for presentation in a later time zone, or to reply to *any* possible religious question) were replaced not by another code but by a person: Jesus.

The old law was replaced not with a new legalism but with freedom.

All of us want to be accepted. But sometimes a tear-catcher must say what is *right* and not just what the tear-sharer wants to hear. We must be prepared to risk rejection, if not ridicule, by those seeking accommodating responses.

When Jeremiah had reservations about this approach, the Lord said, "You must go to everyone I send you to and say whatever I command you. Do not be afraid of them. For I am with you and will rescue you" (Jer. 1:7-8).

Those who catch tears must risk too much, too soon, too little, too late. This skill will be learned through apprenticeship. Some people require milk, Hebrews' author wrote to the early church, while others require meat (5:12); tear-catchers will learn which is appropriate.

On the Outer Banks of North Carolina is a string of lighthouses which warn the ships of dangerous waters and rocks, a critical necessity for maritime commerce. Several years ago, I spent some time vacationing on the

Outer Banks. I had idolized the keepers of these light-houses, ever on guard, right?

I discovered that these friends of sailors were often eccentrics. During the summers their families lived with them, but during the school year the families returned to the coastal towns. So the lightkeepers fought the storms and fogs *alone;* thus some turned to the bottle, especially after close calls.

There was tremendous personal sacrifice for those men to confront the aloneness, to keep the lights on, to keep the ships moving through the waters to the safety of port—not just to protect the cargoes, but the men. They needed a tear-catcher, someone to be with them.

Those who catch tears must risk creating a dependency. So many have refused to help lest it create a dependency— "Then what would I do?"

There are those tear-sharers and tear-catchers who are relationship addicts: "I don't know what I would do without you"; "You're my only friend"; "You're the only person I can turn to." Such declarations stroke the ego and are affirming but can be disarming.

Some tear-catchers have concluded that dependency comes with the territory. A few have used that depen-dency to nourish their own psychological needs. But the ego-stroking may cause tear-catchers to become proud or overconfident or put some on an emotional roller-coaster where they must be immediately reinforced if they are to be effective. Sometimes there will be no praise for the tear-catcher. After all, only one leper returned to thank Jesus (Luke 17:15).

That's one problem with some of the discipleship programs so in vogue today. Perhaps I've seen too many of the excesses and not enough of the triumphs. But the risk is a call to the messianic dimension of personality that unfortunately lies dormant in most tear-catchers. One leader in this process self-righteously stated that he was reproducing himself in another. Jesus did not clone disciples—they were an integrated but varied group: Peter, Thomas, John; very different, yet all disciples.

We can create, then nourish a dependency without knowing it. This is exhibited when a church falls apart after a pastor moves to another assignment or dies. We're so generous in denouncing the quasi- or pseudo-evangelical cults that we ignore the personality cults within main-stream Christianity. This tendency existed in the early church. Paul described the Corinthian Christians as saying, "I follow Paul" or "I follow Apollos." "What, after all, is Apollos?" he responded. "And what is Paul? Only servants" (I Cor. 3:4-5).

We must not develop a network of tear-catchers the way urban politicians once assembled their political machines which, ostensibly, were networks of people to help other people. There is no spiritual pyramiding. We do not franchise tear-catching the way Colonel Sanders franchised fried chicken. There will be no need for organizations to award the equivalent of Oscars or Emmys for the best supporting tear-catcher. And there won't be the need for the tear-catcher-of-the-year award.

The biggest surprise of heaven will be those people whose names or pictures never appeared in the top evangelical magazines, who never appeared on religious TV or did personal appearances at churches, but who will be the saints. During the introductions some of us will surely mutter, "Never heard of him."

The tear-catcher leaves the whole question of reward-recognition to the One who "made himself of no reputation," and "took the very nature of a servant" (Phil. 2:7).

The tear-catcher smiles when he sees the once-wounded overcome the hurt to become a tear-catcher.

I deeply respect those persons who have been my tear-catchers. But as much as I respect them, I cannot become a clone, nor would they want me to be. I can only be Harold Ivan Smith. The call to every tear-catcher is to be yourself, to be authentic.

Admittedly, it is easier to copy, to imitate, than to go through the time-consuming process of development. Yet some settle for being scaled-down versions, little replicas—perhaps unaware of God's desire for their uniqueness.

A TEAR-CATCHER DISCIPLINES REJECTION

When the total picture of tear-catching is presented, some candidates conclude there are other, more desirable enterprises in the kingdom besides tear-catching. "I think I'll sing in the choir."

The pew-warmer may applaud the reports of tear-catching going on in the congregation and fail to hear the call.

We are designed to cry! There is no shortage of incidents which provoke tears. But there is a drastic shortage of people to wipe away tears.

"I can to all things through Christ who strengthens me" is easily memorized. The tear-catcher inserts a qualifier, "I can catch tears through Christ who catches mine."

The tear-catcher is disciplined.

10

THE AGENDA OF A TEAR-CATCHER: CARING, LISTENING, SHARING

We live in an era of what James Ramey termed "isolationships" or "isorelationships."[1] We live with calculated friendships: "I'll do this for you, *if* you'll do ———— in return." Indeed, many of our expectations are not even verbalized, which inevitably leads to confusion or frustration.

There are three ways I can meet you:

1. With my hands folded on my chest and perhaps a hint of a sarcastic snarl on my face, "I dare you to get through to me."

2. With my hands out in front of me to keep you at a safe distance. "Don't come any closer or I'll ————."

3. With my arms wide open although I do not know that you won't try to hit me in the stomach.

We are at the same time starved for friendship and intimacy and yet afraid of it. "Feast or famine" explained one adult of his friendships. There are so few shortcuts to making ourselves vulnerable other than an openness that invites people to walk into our lives. Sometimes we have to leave the gate open.

The willingness to be vulnerable is a crucial dimension for a tear-catcher. The tear-catcher must be willing to risk.

I have been heavily influenced by the writing and life of Dietrich Bonhoeffer, a German pastor and theologian who was killed during World War II. God allowed Bonhoeffer to foresee the outbreak of global war and the ultimate devastation of Germany. He perceived the need for a cadre of pastors, faithful to the Word—not only to preach in Germany after the war but *during* the war as well.

Bonhoeffer did not mince words with Hitler or with those German pastors who aligned themselves with the Third Reich. His friends in England and in the United States, obviously aware of the consequences of his clashes with Hitler, helped him leave Germany by offering the safety of a classroom-pulpit in England. After a few months, he decided to return to Germany.

He increased the pace of his anti-Hitler tactics and was forced underground. His American friends, after the outbreak of war in 1939, secured a position for Bonhoeffer at Union Theological Seminary in New York; another port of safety. He served for a while but again longed for Germany, and returned home to share with fellow Christians the struggle against Hitler. Out of his struggles came *The Cost of Discipleship,* which condemned "cheap grace." Bonhoeffer talked of a costly grace that demanded something of the believer. Prison made the theologian into a tear-catcher. In the last days of his life in Tegel prison, Bonhoeffer wandered from cell to cell comforting the prisoners as the waves of Allied planes bombed Germany.

Four tenets of Bonhoeffer's theology are worth consideration here. These come from his small book *Life Together.*

Jesus Christ lived in the midst of his enemies.

The believer feels no shame, as though he were still living too much in the flesh, when he yearns for the physical presence of other Christians.

We belong to one another only in and through Jesus Christ. . . . A Christian needs others because of Jesus Christ.

God has willed that we should seek and find His living Word in the witness of a brother. . . . The Christian needs another Christian who speaks God's Word to him.[2]

By substituting the term *tear-catcher* into Bonhoeffer's writing we formulate an agenda.

One is a [tear-catcher] to another only through Jesus Christ. I am a [tear-catcher] to another person through what Jesus Christ did for me and to me; the other person has become a [tear-catcher] to me through what Jesus Christ did for him.[3]

Thus Christ opened up the way to God and the way to our brothers and sisters.

Of course, because we are human, it is possible to be disappointed by a brother or sister, even by another tear-catcher. Bonhoeffer would perhaps have suggested that tear-catching is not an idea we must realize, but "a reality created by God in Christ in which we may participate."[4]

Let's examine the agenda of a tear-catcher.

TEAR-CATCHERS CARE

"They'll Know We Are Christians by Our Love" is a popular Christian folksong of the sixties. It's easily memorized, easily hummed, but somewhat difficult to practice.

"No one cares what happens to me" protests a teen or an elderly grandmother. In the Age of the Me, *my* me is more important than *your* me. So it becomes a question of whose me we're talking about.

Have you ever heard a pagan say, "I am carrying such a burden"? Probably not. "The brother is a burden to the Christian, precisely because he is a Christian. For the pagan the other person never becomes a burden at all. He simply sidesteps every burden that others may impose on him."[5]

A tear-catcher cares when it is convenient and when it is inconvenient.

> God sometimes asks us
> > quite simply
> > to abandon the security
> > of the comfortable
> > and the safe
> To walk with him
> > to one
> > who needs our care.

The tear-catcher is also asked to abandon the safety of the first person singular (or plural) to care for another. Some would-be tear-catchers can hardly wait for the sharer to take a breath so they can break into the conversation flow. Warren Farrell observed:

> We listen to the first sentence or two a person makes, assume we know what is to follow, and start forming our own story related to our own accomplishments (or ego) while the other person is still talking.
>
> We often generally drop in a credential (to further support our position) and end the story with a reference to ourself which encourages the group to focus on what we have brought up rather than return to the first talker.[6]

The psalmist commented, "Reproach has broken my heart, and I am so sick. And I looked for sympathy, but there was none; And for comforters, but I found none" (Ps. 69:20 NASV). Through caring we stand in the shadow of the Cross. "Carry each other's burdens" (Gal. 6:2) is an invitation to tear-catching.

> A tear
> however salty
> is always
> an invitation.

How heavy are tears anyway? Why, even someone with a bad back could easily carry tears; they only weigh down the one who sheds them.

It's easy to catch the tears of those we love and those who love us. However, the words of Jesus come into focus: "Whatever you did for one of the least of these brothers of mine, you did for me" (Matt. 25:40). The least of them includes:

- the boisterous
- the offensive
- the guilty
- those "in deep sin"
- those who have committed what we consider to be the three-star sins

and those who reject our tear-catching and snarl, "Go away and leave me alone."

> Catching the tears of the smallest pilgrim
> is as important a task
> as a man could face.

Remember the words of the author of the Letter to the Hebrews (Heb. 13:2) about entertaining angels unaware; who knows but the beggar's tears are for you to catch? And if you refuse, who will?

> Can I be so busy
>   that I ignore
>   another's tears
> but become impatient
>   when no one
>   notices mine?

TEAR-CATCHERS LISTEN

"He never heard a word I said" and "In one ear, out the other" are common expressions in our society. Kaiser Medical Group in California has discovered that many wives complain that their husbands are hard of hearing. Test results show the husbands are *tired* of hearing. They do not want to hear what their wives are saying and act out a hearing loss.

In *Healing the Pain of Everyday Loss,* Dr. Ira Tanner observed that "hearing is not the same as listening," although we use the terms as synonyms. It is possible "to hear someone's words without listening to the feelings behind the words."[7]

Most people do not need highly skilled professionals in psychiatry or psychology. However, they *hire* people-helpers because the significant people in their lives are not listening. Much of our professional care is in fact a luxury of an overabundant economic but spiritually impoverished society. Thus we have created what amounts to mental health "seven-elevens." If only those we love would listen to us!

And we would be enriched by listening. I think this is one element contributing to the poverty of children today.

On Sundays my family went visiting—and we sometimes visited people who did not have children my age or any children at all. So I sat and listened to the richness of the adult conversations (children were to be seen and not heard in those days). Today's teens generally have significant conversations only with their peers.

Somehow this conversational fear may be related to dating. I remember the arrival tactics for a date included having as little time as possible to sit and talk with her parents while she finished combing her hair. The father asked questions like, "What does your father do?" You often thought he was on a fishing expedition to determine your stability as a date—"Any history of any of the following in your family (just nod): insanity? depravity? bankruptcy? drunkenness?"

Often the mother responded with comments like "That's nice" to every other answer until on the high sign she rushed off to see "what's keeping her."

Some fathers were so experienced they could rattle off questions like the district attorney. And there came that moment of relief when you walked down the porch steps with your date.

But how is it that the couple who talked for hours while dating seldom talk about important issues of the heart anymore?

How many spouses listen to their mates while reading the paper or while watching television? Listening involves the eyes as well as the ears and a recognition of what was *not* said as much as what was said.

Traditionally, this is hard for male tear-catchers to master. Women are much more prepared to be listeners. My mother could hold a conversation with the wrong number. However, my dad's approach in telephone conversations was

1. Tell them what he wants to tell them;
2. Tell them;
3. Tell them what he told them.

It's too easy to nod and "uh-huh" our way through a conversation. Then comes the moment when we lack some details and must call and ask, "Now, refresh my memory," and hopefully the incident or detail will become clearer. Bonhoeffer concluded: "The first service that one owes to others in the fellowship consists of listening to them. Just as love to God begins with listening to His Word, so the beginning of love for the brethren is learning to listen to them.[8]

Bonhoeffer concluded, "He who can no longer listen to his brother will soon no longer be listening to God.[9]

> How many times have I
>   approached
>   the suffering/the hurting
>   like one of Job's "friends"?
> Have I swapped doctor's stories
>   or drug names
>   or side effects
>   rather than listened?
> Have I been so busy
>   insisting
>   that "I understand"
>   that
>   you're more alone
>   during my visit
>   than after I've gone?

Rudolph E. Grantham has developed some listening helps that will be valuable to the tear-catcher.

Concentrate on the person who is speaking. The speaker often arouses similar feelings in the listener. The tear-catcher then might respond to his or her own feelings instead of to the speaker's.

Find out what the problem is. Where is the tear-sharer hurting the most?

Repeat what you hear the person saying and feeling. "Do I hear you saying . . . ?" "Did I understand you correctly?"

Respond to the message that seems to be the most important to the speaker. If verbalizing deepens depression, try to help the person think of resources and personal strengths that might be of help in dealing with the problem.

Ask questions to clarify details. This lets the tear-sharer know you're interested.

Summarize the message. This will reduce the replaying of what you have already heard.

Resist curiosity. "Curiosity," Grantham says, "is one's own self-interest seeking information." Not only did curiosity kill the cat; it also has paralyzed many potential tear-catchers.

Determine the goals of the listening relationship. "How can I help you?"[10]

It is easy to say, "Tell me more," because some people use gossip to inflate the ego or to appear that they know everything that's going on.

A final point is *declare the confidentiality*. Naturally, the tear-sharer will add a disclaimer, "Please don't tell anyone that I told you about —— and some listeners can respond by gesture or touch and affirm, "I won't tell a soul" which translates, "Boy, wait till Helen hears about this!" After confessional listening, the time is appropriate for a reassuring promise of silence.

There will always be a shortage of listeners.

TEAR-CATCHERS SHARE

One of our first struggles in life is to learn to share, whether it is our M&M's, our toys, or whatever. Many parents and children collide on the definition of *mine*. It may have been mine, but if I was ordered to share, I quickly learned not to protest too much.

Bill Gaither's phrase has captured our thinking, "When one has a heartache, we all shed a tear."[11] That is the common denominator of Christian friendship. And that was the dynamic of the early church. "All the believers were together and *had everything in common.* Selling their possessions and goods, they gave *to anyone* as he had need" (Acts 2:44-45, italics mine). Dare we think Luke was overenthusiastic when he wrote, "There were no needy persons among them" (Acts 4:34)? A lot of Christians have trouble reconciling those verses with capitalism.

Remember when Peter was entering the temple to pray and was stopped by a beggar? He responded, "I have no silver or gold, but what I have I give you" (Acts 3:6). It is so easy to reach into our wallets rather than into our time. This is the beauty of God's plan of tear-catching: the poorest widow with a telephone can listen to someone share tears.

My Grandmother Baker survived on a meager income primarily of Social Security benefits. Every year she scrimped and gave me a box of chocolate-covered cherries. I don't know how much they cost, but it involved a sacrifice. And she never asked a lot from me.

When I got married we picked out china, silver patterns—in short, went the whole route of bridal registration. Later, it seemed ironic that those items had once seemed so essential. In the years we were married we used the stuff only a few times.

Well, my grandmother couldn't afford that stuff. But years before she had made a quilt for each of her grandsons. When I married I got my quilt—a purple Dutch-boy pattern. I never thought of it as worth a great deal—it was just something Grandmother had made.

Then one day I took it to a dry cleaners and a man started offering me all this money for the quilt. Every "no" raised the ante until I heard myself say, "What do you mean, how much will I take? Why, my grandmother made this for me!"

That quilt means a lot to me now; it's kept me warm on many cold winter nights. She shared something of herself. No doubt she prayed for me while she stitched. That's the essence of sharing.

Sometimes sharing means sharing the wealth; at other times it may mean sharing a meal or perhaps information. "Just wanted you to know about" some special event that a friend would enjoy but otherwise might have missed. Have you ever said a day late, "I *almost* called you, but I thought surely you knew about it"?

In another dimension we share recipes. At Christmas when I bake sugar cookies, I use the recipe that has been handed down by the Smiths and Eckerts and Plues and so forth. Sometimes I have enjoyed a dish and have expressed interest in getting the recipe. Many hosts have not only shared the recipe, but assured me that I could make it successfully. "If I can do it, so can you!" The affirmation may be as important as the recipe!

It's easy to develop sharing from a self-interest perspective. "Who are our allies?" asks a nation in distributing its foreign aid. "What's in it for me?" can be subliminal and yet build barriers.

I am reminded of the story of II Kings when a widow appealed to the prophet Elisha. Her debtors wanted to foreclose and seize her two sons as payment for her deceased husband's debts (II Kings 4:1-7). She was wringing her hands asking, "What am I gonna do?" Some would have referred her to a social worker. But Elisha responded, "How can I help you?" and then confounded her by asking, "What do you have in your house?"

The woman must have thought, "Is he deaf? If I had something in my house, why would I be here?" She reported that she had nothing at all . . . well, "except a little oil."

Elisha instructed her to go to all of her neighbors and borrow vessels. "Don't ask for just a few." She must have wondered about his wisdom. Here I am with a man coming to collect my two boys and I am out collecting jars! Some advice!

However, she obeyed his request and gathered the vessels, went into her home, and shut the door. And Elisha began praying. She began pouring the oil into the vessels. Amazingly the oil filled all the jars. Then the oil was sold and the debt paid.

The significant point is that had the neighbors been asked to contribute cash, the boys would have been sold. But they gave what they had and thus helped solve the widow's predicament.

Tear-catchers share sometimes in what seem unorthodox or unusual ways. Ben Patterson tells a story in *The Wittenburg Door.*

> I went through what amounted to two broken engagements over a five-year period—with the same girl. When it was all over forever and I knew it, I went to visit a close friend who had been intimately acquainted with the details of everything that had happened during that painful and stormy period of my life. I was numb and tired of hurting. We talked for a while and when I got up to leave he suggested that we pray together. I prayed first and then waited for him to begin. Nothing came for a long time. I was about to ask what was wrong when I heard something. It was a sob. Cliff was weeping for me when I could no longer weep for myself. There have been few times in my life when I have felt as comforted. He was a little bit of the Holy Spirit to me at that moment. [12]

Paul instructed, "Each of you should look not only to your own interests, but also to the interests of others" (Phil. 2:4). Apparently that verse was overlooked by the rural farmer who prayed, "O Lord, bless my four and no more!"

SUMMARY

The agenda of the tear-catcher involves caring, listening, and sharing. There is no cheap tear-catching. These activities can be inconvenient; but then it was Jesus who said, "If anyone would come after me, he must deny himself" (Mark 8:34).

11

THE AGENDA OF A TEAR-CATCHER: ENCOURAGING, HELPING, CONFRONTING

In the previous chapter, we noted three items on the tear-catcher's agenda: caring, listening, and sharing. In this chapter we turn to three other components: encouraging, helping, and confronting. I would point out that their order in this book, with the exception of "confronting," is not significant. Some tear-catchers are better at one agenda item than another.

TEAR-CATCHERS ENCOURAGE

The old cowboy classic "Home on the Range" provides one well-memorized line, "Where seldom is heard a discouraging word and the skies are not cloudy all day." The people in little country churches used to sing a religious parallel of that thought, "The Unclouded Day."

We live in the age of the put-down, an "art form" mastered by comedian Don Rickles. We lift ourselves up by putting others down. Many would protest that it's a dog-eat-dog-world out there. And the cold, cruel world produces casualties. The human junk pile grows higher every day.

In staff meeting one day all the reports from staff members had been so negative that our boss finally asked,

"Doesn't anyone have any encouraging news to report?" The temptation was to make up something so the meeting could end on a positive note. At the opposite end of the scale, tear-catchers are encouragers; they see something good in everything. Sometimes it is a question of changing the angle of one's perspective or making a decision to see the good.

We need to encourage one another, as the writer of Hebrews suggested: "Let us do all we can to help one another's faith" (10:25 Phillips; "encouraging one another" RSV). It only takes a word, a sentence, a note, or a smile.

Sometimes we do not know when we encourage. I have never forgotten a tear-catcher named Lee Woolery who encouraged me to write as we were sitting in his home in Goodlettsville, Tennessee. I doubt that he fully understood the impact of his suggestion. After I left his home, I stopped at a mall and purchased three spiral notebooks. The next day more than half of what became my first book, *Warm Reflections,* had been scribbled into one of those notebooks.

But once it was in those notebooks, I doubted that it was worth anything. Eventually an English professor named Preston Woodruff read the manuscript. I awaited his critique with fear. When he returned the manuscript I noticed stars on the upper right-hand corners of some of the pages.

"Those are the ones I think you should submit," he explained. Based on his encouragement I began a final editing. Ten publishers later, however, came the third influencer, my friend Bob Blocker. One morning he casually asked, "How are things going?" The only thing I could report was that another publisher had turned down my poetry. He suggested a publisher I had not yet tried.

"Ah, they would never publish it," I responded.

"Hey, all you will lose is the postage to find out." Six months later, I signed a contract with that publisher. I am a published writer only because of those three tear-catchers, who encouraged me at every step.

At major intersections of our lives, we often discover a tear-catcher who will encourage us. Paul Tournier noted:

> The riches of life are in those decisive moments when one's life was turned in a new direction. In every life there are a few special moments that count for more than all the rest because they meant the taking of a stand, a self-commitment, a decisive choice.[1]

Too often in moments or seasons of failure, we are tempted to kick the ground in despair. But it's not so much a question of whether or not you fall—but how long you lie there.

A host of people, with the help of an encourager, have found yesterday's defeat adequate fertilizer for tomorrow's dreams. But there are others, without an encourager, who have lain immobilized in the stale, damp ashes of yesterday.

If a pro football player misses an important pass, does he lie kicking the artificial turf? Is that what he is paid $100,000 a season to do? No, his fellow players and sometimes his opponents pull him up and he heads back to the huddle to try again. Babe Ruth, the great home run king, also had a terrific strikeout average!

Tear-catchers are encouragers.

TEAR-CATCHERS HELP

Paul wrote, "In the church God has appointed . . . those able to help others" (I Cor. 12:28). To the Roman believers he suggested, "Share with God's people who are in need. Practice hospitality" (Rom. 12:13).

We live in such busy times. Bonhoeffer said, "We must be ready to *allow* ourselves to be interrupted by God. God will be constantly crossing our path and canceling our plans by sending us people with claims and petitions."[2]

Paul noted, "There are different kinds of gifts, but the same Spirit . . . different kinds of service, but the same Lord" (I Cor. 12:4, 5). It is through the work of the Holy Spirit that we become sensitive to those needs. That was the thought behind the old gospel hymn, "Brighten the corner where you are." It's so romantic to imagine ourselves fighting off lions, tigers, and stampeding elephants to do the Lord's will in Africa. Yet an adult apartment complex in America is as much a mission field as a kraal in Africa. Our mission field is all around us, and the tear-catcher is sensitive to that awareness.

In the early church there arose a dispute over the care of the Aramaic-speaking widows. Some charged that the Grecian widows were treated better. The Apostles, sensitive to the potential for hurt feelings, responded that though "it would not be right for us to neglect the ministry of the word of God in order to wait on tables," since God had called them to preach the Christians should choose seven men who were "known to be full of the Spirit and wisdom" (Acts 6:2-3) to take over the ministry of handing out food. The men who were chosen were not second-class spiritual servants; they had the same qualifications as the apostles.

Dr. W. E. McCumber wrote a sensitive editorial in the *Herald of Holiness.* In an age of leadership conferences and management seminars, he suggested,

We need to arrange a servanthood conference, with workshops in love, forgiveness, feet-washing, cross bearing—in short, workshops in Christlikeness.

God is not waiting for people to get big enough to use, but to get small enough in their own eyes for Him to entrust with His mission and Spirit.

Christ cannot be represented by swaggering leaders who "lord it over" the flock of God. He cannot be represented by puffed-up laymen who nominate themselves as church bosses. He can be honestly manifested only in the lives of those who feel, as did Paul, that they are "less than the least of all the saints."[3]

"I'd really like to help, but . . ." is seldom part of the tear-catcher's vocabulary. "How *can* I help?" is more likely. Most tear-catchers are willing to rearrange, to postpone, to delay their own agenda to meet the needs of others. Even Jesus was criticized in this regard. En route to heal Jairus's daughter, he stopped when he felt his healing virtue touch someone. He asked, "Who touched me?" Noting the press of the crowd, the disciples thought he was kidding. Because of the interruption, however, Jesus was delayed. Jairus, the grieving father, was told by someone who had just come from his house, "Your daughter is dead. Don't bother the teacher any more" (Luke 8:49). Yet Jesus responded, "Don't be afraid; just believe" (8:50). The girl was healed.

The tear-catcher helps by noting that what we think is peculiar to us (or qualifies us for living martyrdom) is common to all human beings (I Cor. 10:13). The enemy attempts to insulate us from those who would catch our tears. "What would they think *if they knew*?" (three of the most paralyzing words in the English language). Sometimes our masquerades of self-sufficiency encourage others to presume that we do not need them. Thus we sabotage ourselves by going it alone.

Jesus could have gone alone to Gethsemane, but he chose three friends to accompany him in that awesome hour.

TEAR-CATCHERS CONFRONT

After we have built a relationship with someone through

- caring
- listening
- sharing
- encouraging
- helping

then we have a right to confront.

"Are you sticking your nose into my business?" my brother asked me on more than one occasion. The process of butting in generally lets us quickly discover where we stand with another individual. Confrontation, however, is the positive side of butting in. Tanner calls it "responsible confrontation" or "knowing when to confront." It is a skill requiring wisdom, tact, and compassion.[4]

It also requires courage. And we are cowardly at times, afraid to confront. "The time wasn't right," we say, or "I chickened out at the last minute." (And then it's easy to blame ourselves. "I had my chance and blew it.") Those moments in which we are deciding whether or not to confront seem like an eternity. Reasons not to confront abound. Yet, "Why should we be afraid of one another," Bonhoeffer asked, "since both of us have only God to fear? Why should we think that our brother would not understand us, when we understood very well what was meant when somebody spoke God's comfort or God's admonition to us, perhaps in words that were halting and unskilled?"[5]

How Christian is it to deprive another of the help he or she needs and that we can give? The basis on which we relate to one another is the event of the Cross which reconciles us to each other. Therefore we are to "speak the truth in love." That can be a difficult assignment.

It is easier to comfort than to confront. Yet if we care enough to confront, we can make a difference. Sometimes people get stuck in their grief, in their tears. On those occasions the skilled tear-catcher "must confront . . . them to get on with grief, even to jar them out of self-pity and morbidness."[6]

In one seminar a woman asked, "How long does it take to get over a mate's death?"

"As long as you decide," I replied. When her eyebrows suggested she didn't care for that answer, I decided to probe a bit. "Where's your husband's watch?"

"On the nightstand beside the bed where he left it the night he died," she confessed. I learned that his suits still hung in the closet; his folded shirts lay in the drawers. Everything was just the way he left it seven years before.

She had become a victim of the invisible chains of grief; someone had to confront her in order to comfort her. In order to get over her husband's death, she had to let go of that relationship. Confronting is hard to do, but we can do it without betraying the quality of the relationship.

Confrontation can save later embarrassment; it can be preventive. How many times have you remarked, "I wish someone had told me that then," or ". . . before now"? Because no one did, the present burden is heavier.

Unfortunately, too many people use confrontation in an attempt to stab the tear-sharer in the quick. When I was a child, evangelists came to our church periodically. They preached a rugged gospel that frightened me because I could never live up to those high, exacting standards. They made such harsh, confrontative statements that it took weeks and months (even years) to get over their visits. Apparently, they thought it was their task to preach on subjects the pastor avoided. My dad called the process "skinning 'em." That kind of premature, insensitive confrontation can be counterproductive.

Many witnesses for the Lord have been ineffective because they alienated the one who needed the witness. "You said ———! Don't deny it. I heard you!" "You do ———, and it's wrong!" Such intense, accusative statements send people scampering for a shield behind which to hide. As children we had an expression around our house when our parents were about to discover something we assumed (and preferred) they did not know. "Boy, you're in trouble *now*," or "You're gonna be in the doghouse now." Unfortunately we often continue to use such statements as adults, with the result that people are put on the defensive.

Tear-catchers have decided their task is to help get people out of the doghouse, not put them in. Through the leadership of the Holy Spirit, they are sensitive to needs as well as to timing.

One of the most remarkable stories I have ever heard concerned a wife whose husband had deserted her for a woman much younger. The wife was at her wit's end. Then the thought occurred to her that she should bake her husband's favorite dessert and take it over to the other woman's apartment where he was now living. With a great deal of concern, she obeyed those thoughts.

When the woman did not answer the door, she left the dessert. A few days later she was prompted to repeat the experience. This time, she noticed a slight flutter of curtains as she approached, but no one answered the door.

The third time she felt so prompted, the door opened and the new woman of her husband's dreams stood eyeballing her. "Why are you trying to poison us?" she demanded.

"Poison you?" the wife responded.

"It's no telling what's in *that* . . . arsenic or rat poison."

"No. It's Jim's favorite dessert. I just want him to be happy, and so I thought I would bring this over." Then, to the wife's surprise, the younger woman invited her in, and they talked over coffee.

To make a long story short, the husband returned to his wife. Her gentle confrontation convinced him of the rare wife he had.

Confrontation involves not only what is said and done but also how it is said and done. Tone of voice, for example, is extremely important. It's too easy to use King James language or stained-glass voices. Sometimes too the tear-sharer accuses us (rightfully) of being holier than thou. We come across like the Pharisee who prayed, "God, I thank thee that I am not like this ————" sinner, person with problems, etc. As Jesus noted, it is easier to get the splinter out of our brother's eye than to remove the beam in ours (Luke 6:42).

How do we distinguish between confrontation and judging? We are specifically told not to judge "or you too will be judged" (Matt. 7:1). Paul tells us we can be condemned by what we approve (Rom. 14:22). He wrote to the Romans, "You, therefore, have no excuse, you who pass judgment on someone else, for at whatever point you judge the other, you are condemning yourself, because you who pass judgment do the same things" (2:1).

In other words, that which we cannot stand in others often represents a weakness within us. That's the wisdom of James: "Not many of you should presume to be teachers, my brothers, because you know that we who teach [or catch tears] will be judged more strictly. *We all stumble in many ways*" (James 3:1-2, italics mine).

The characteristic that distinguishes confrontation from judgment is the knowledge that "we all stumble in many ways." Tear-catchers know that. They know that they are part of the community of the forgiven and the *forgiving.* They are to share the good news of forgiveness because they know what God has forgiven in them.

If we confront, we *must* be motivated by the Holy Spirit who goes before us. We must be "pure; then peace-loving, considerate, submissive, full of mercy and good fruit, impartial and sincere" (James 3:17). Certainly some will misjudge our motive or intent. But there are those whose lives are different because someone cared enough to confront them. George Bernard Shaw once quipped, "The worst sin towards our fellow creatures is not to hate them but to be indifferent to them."[7]

Take my own case, for example. I have a weight problem and some time ago I ballooned up to 275 pounds. My self-concept disappeared. "How could anyone love a fat slob like me?" I angrily demanded of the mirror. I began to avoid mirrors but not calories. Finally a track coach named Norm Witek said to me, "You're disgusting! Each time I see you you're bigger than the last time. When are you going to do something about your weight?"

Naturally my feelings were hurt. That was easy for him to say. He could eat anything he wanted (and as much) and never gain a pound.

But there came a day when I looked up Coach Witek and admitted that I needed his help. He started me jogging and in the last eight years I've missed very few days. But I'd lost weight before and always gained it back . . . this could be just another fad, unless . . . But Norm thought I could do it. One way he helped me after he confronted me was that he often ran with me, encouraging me to set a longer goal, then another.

Today I weigh ninety-five pounds less than I did eight years ago when Norm confronted me. I'm glad that he risked the confrontation.

Norm risked what was then a shallow friendship but has earned a lasting loyalty. I couldn't believe in myself, but Norm did.

> In the lexicon of heaven
> there is only one synonym
> for caring: risk!

CONCLUSION

To be a tear-catcher, one needs to care, to listen, to share, to encourage, to help, and to confront. Being a tear-catcher is to act in the spirit of an old gospel song:

Throw out the lifeline across the dark wave.
There is a brother whom someone should save.
Somebody's brother! Oh, who then will dare
To throw out the lifeline, his peril to share?

Throw out the lifeline! Throw out the lifeline!
Someone is drifting away.
Throw out the lifeline! Throw out the lifeline!
Someone is sinking today.[8]

We must be alert to open doors and opportunities to catch tears. Tear-catching is designed to be not a profession but a passion, fueled by our continual awareness of all the "somebody's brothers and sisters" in need.

Of course, it would be easy to set up "Tear-Catchers International," as a nonprofit ministry. Then we would have to have

- a post office box
- a newsletter

- a mailing list
- stationery
- a logo
- a board of directors
- a budget

The ministry would become formalized—we would have to be concerned about our image, especially when we went on television. But Jesus didn't have any of these essentials for his ministry. I've wondered sometimes what kind of stationery he would have chosen. How high would the back of his chair have been if he'd set up his nonprofit business? Can't you see him poring over a computer printout of his contributors?

> Why is it that testimonies become
> "ministries"
> nonprofit corporations
> and then monuments
> which can continue
> after the testimony has ended?

Jesus did not need any of these items to confront and comfort a woman (five times divorced) at a Samaritan well. He merely asked her for a drink of water and began a conversation with her. Some of the citizens of heaven are there because "many of the Samaritans from that town believed in him *because of the woman's testimony*" (John 4:39, italics mine). One confrontation on one afternoon decided the eternal destinies of several people. Who knows what difference your care could make?

The agenda of a tear-catcher is not that difficult to determine. It is, however, difficult to follow. We get excited and anxious to take giant steps, overlooking the next small step that needs to be taken.

One paragraph in an article in *The Upper Room Disciplines* caught my attention: "Our eyes can be so focused on the great ends that we are incapable of seeing opportunities for witness [or tear-catching] right beside us. Our goals can be so grandiose and distant that we fail to see particular human need at our doorstep."[9]

All we're asked to do is catch tears—so simple and in God's design so profound. That's quite an agenda.

Are you willing to be a tear-catcher?

12

THE FUTURE OF TEAR-CATCHING

There will always be a future for tear-catchers; the need for them will never grow less and so the shortage of them will never be eliminated. Through the enlistment of new tear-catchers, the waiting can be reduced, at least slightly. In the tough days that are surely ahead, the task of the tear-catcher may well be to stand with one foot in hell and, despite the smoke, prophesy of hope.

In these moments tear-catchers dare not enjoy the luxury of pie-in-the-sky-in-the-bye-and-bye, although certainly they believe in heaven. Rather, there is much to be accomplished in the here and now that will determine where people will spend their bye and bye.

How do tear-catchers perceive the future? There is a mentality that sees the future as the last hand, not unlike a card game. All that remains is to play the last hand and to count the cards. In games that is a reality because there are a precise number of cards; however, in terms of the future, such is not the case. We don't know the precise number of cards still to be played.

The Scripture points out that "*No one* knows the hour or day," when Christ will come again. One must surely wonder what keeps the Lord from saying, "That's it! Pull the plug!" in an encore of his decision in Genesis 6.

However, we do know the nature of God—that he is a God of order and patience. He is not manipulated by humans.

He longs for that moment when the church will shed its adolescence and become what he designed it to be: a cadre of tear-catchers who make a difference through the leadership of the Holy Spirit.

The future of the tear-catcher always offers an opportunity, an invitation to abandon the systematic or familiar in order to minister—to remain simply a tear-catcher, however chaotic the times will become.

There are no slogans or seasonal goals for tear-catchers other than a day-in, day-out commitment: to catch tears when convenient, when inconvenient.

Tear-catchers who have prepared for today's tomorrow have learned to manage their fears. Our Heavenly Father is not intimidated by our confession, "I'm afraid." In his strength we can walk through the marketplace and through academia, the religious communities, and the ghettos scratching through the small "hopes" printed or scrawled on the walls of our world in order to insert a capital *H*. Hope always begins with a capital *H*. And that one gesture of faith, when viewed by the weariest or weakest pilgrim, will spawn a breath of fresh air. We must proclaim, "I dare to Hope!"

There will be those whom we must ask to repeat that phrase with us: "I too dare to Hope."

THE FUTURE DEMANDS A COMMITMENT FROM THE TEAR-CATCHER

There is an old hymn of the church that speaks to the point—"A Charge to Keep I Have,"

To serve the present age,
My calling to fulfill;

O may it all my powers engage
To do my Master's will!

That is easier sung than lived. For with us are those who long for the safety of yesterday, those who wish to turn back. When the great wagon trains crossed the heartland of the American continent, there were those who gave up the dream and stopped where they were: that place became "the promised land" or an amended version.

The Lord of the future beckons to us as he did to Peter, to walk toward him, to trust. What would have happened if the majority of the disciples had not chosen the safety of the boat but had gone over the side with Peter? This is the day for which we have prepared; there are those who will shed tears today that we can catch.

THE FUTURE CONDITIONS THE TEAR-CATCHER

Hopefully, a generation who saw their parents' fear of tears will not merely mimic their decision. Soon a generation will weep as easily as laugh, understanding that both are human expressions.

And a generation of males, unintimidated by their own tears, will make an impact upon our society's thinking. "And each man will teach his children" the beauty of tears.

And a generation of children will grow to maturity without having been scolded or teased; tears will be their friends.

The tear-catcher must be challenged to go beyond the convenient, safe parameters and into the night where people weep.

TEAR-CATCHERS WILL ALWAYS BE VIEWED SKEPTICALLY

"It's too good to be true, so I don't want to get my hopes up. I might be disappointed." That's the mind-set of a lot of people. They desperately want someone to catch their tears, but they are skeptical.

So there will be the taunts, the curses, the rejections, but these must not be used as proof of our martyrdom!

As our culture plunges further into the spectacle, the auto-pleasurable, the deification of the first person singular, that thirst for wholeness will again surface. Within the heart there will always be a craving to find, to meet an authentic person, whether male or female, young or old, who would catch our tears.

Tear-catchers will be hard pressed to keep up the demands. It will become increasingly easier for tear-catchers to burn out, especially if they pride themselves on their own strength. Tear-catchers will need more time-outs, more times to share their own tears.

Yet that which was promised so long ago to Isaiah is available to the tear-catcher.

> He gives strength to the weary
>   and increases the power of the weak.
> Even youths grow tired and weary,
>   and young men stumble and fall;
> But those who hope in the Lord
>   will renew their strength.
> They will soar on wings like eagles;
>   they will run and not grow weary,
>   they will walk and not be faint. (Isa. 40:29-31)

People will ask more, expect more, even *demand* more of the tear-catcher. There will be those recruits who cannot make the grade, who will find the commitment exhausting.

Yet, somewhere en route, we will become the people of God. That longing for a "rootedness" will touch the emotionstream of the soul and prosper.

> For the tear-catcher
> has chosen
> to believe
> in a tomorrow
> that begins today.

BUT TEAR-CATCHERS HAVE THE PROMISE OF GOD'S TOUCH

There will surely come that moment of moments in eternity's day when tear-catchers from every tribe, every tongue, every race will gather in the presence of The Tear-Catcher.

> I believe in a Christmas future
> when all of God's children
> will be home.
> I believe that in our first moments
> in his presence
> We will realize
> how much he gave
> to spend those years among us
> in order
> to invite us
> to spend Forever with him.
> His coming
> locked this world
> into a loving embrace.
> He asks us to strengthen the grip.

There is a legend that the One whose birth inaugurated Christmas has never celebrated that event but awaits that certain dawn when the same angel band who sang to shepherds will again be assembled to sing.

> In that incredible moment
> tear-catchers from every tongue
> will join in on the chorus
> and somehow we will all understand.
> And even Dr. Handel will be speechless
> at that rendition
> of the Hallelujah Chorus.

Then the lineup will start. It is required if Revelation 7:17 and 21:4 are fulfilled. "He will wipe every tear from their eyes." In eternity, "there will be no more death or mourning or crying or pain" (21:4).

Just being there would produce tears: for those who came from the lion's den, from the prisons, from persecution, and from those of us who have lived quiet, normal lives.

Genesis proclaims, "In the beginning God . . ." (1:1). Genesis reports that God said, "Let there be ————" and there were oceans and seas, the seasons, the mountains, night and day, creatures and wild animals. God *spoke* our world into existence. So in that first moment in heaven, why doesn't he just ring a bell and announce "No more tears"? With the wave of his hand, the lacrimals would be as dry as the Sahara. Or God could have the angels post signs throughout heaven, "No crying, please."

The God who by the wave of his hand flung the stars to the darkest regions of the night, who put the world into place, will *personally* wipe away every tear. That's the promise of Revelation 7:17. I do not know how long that process will take, but everyone will be entitled to a place in line.

Well, I hate waiting in lines, but when it is important enough, I wait.

The most important thing I will ever do is take my place in that line. And however long it will have taken for me to make it to the head of the line will seem unimportant when I hear the word *next*.

By the act of Jesus Christ, The Tear-Catcher, the Lion of Judah, I have the possibility of standing in God's presence. And he will touch my chin and gently trace his hand across my forehead. And in that split second the lacrimal glands will not dry up but disappear, and God will say, "Welcome home."

I can only anticipate that moment through watching a loving parent wipe tears from a child's eyes; of sensing a hand around the shoulder, of hearing the words, "Don't cry."

That is the future for tear-catchers—a moment, yet to be.

> And the last tears of the saints
>   will be collected
>   to create
>   the fountains of heaven.

NOTES

2. THE ANATOMY OF A TEAR

1. William F. Evans, *Anatomy and Physiology: The Basic Principles* (Englewood Cliffs, N.J.: Prentice-Hall, 1971), pp. 283, 398.
2. Arthur S. Freese, *The Miracle of Vision* (New York: Harper & Row, 1977), pp. 18-19.
3. *Stedman's Medical Dictionary*, 22d ed. (Baltimore: Williams & Wilkins, 1972), p. 147.
4. Conrad G. Mueller and Mae Randolph, *Light and Vision*, a volume of the *Life Science Library* (New York: Time, 1966), p. 26.
5. Ben Esterman, *The Eye Book: A Specialist's Guide to Your Eyes and Their Care* (Arlington, Va.: Great Oceans Publishing Co., 1977), pp. 216-28.
6. Marcel Monnier, *Functions of the Nervous System* (Amsterdam: Elsevier Publishing Co, 1968), pp. 574-575.
7. Freese, p. 43; Mollie S. Smart and Russell C. Smart, *Infants: Development and Relationships* (New York: Macmillan, 1973), p. 80.
8. Freese, p. 18.
9. Ibid., p. 42.
10. Esterman, p. 217.

3. THE MOTIVATION OF A TEAR

1. Monnier, *Functions of the Nervous System*, p. 575.
2. Helmuth Plessner, *Laughing and Crying: A Study of the Limits of Human Behavior*, trans. James Spencer Churchill and Marjorie Green (Evanston, Ill.: Northwestern University Press, 1970), p. 56.

4. THE REGIMENT OF SPECTATORS

1. "Entrevista De La Puerta," *The Wittenburg Door* 56 (August-September 1980): 13.

2. Charles R. Swindoll, *Three Steps Forward, Two Steps Back* (Nashville: Thomas Nelson, 1980).

5. CALL OUT THE MILITIA

1. Earl Lee, "Please . . . Let Us Do It," *Herald of Holiness* 59 (15 January 1980): 11.
2. Gary R. Collins, "Popular Psychology: Short-cut Solutions?" *Christianity Today* (2 May 1980), pp. 19-22.

6. RECOGNIZING THOSE WHO CANNOT ASK FOR HELP

1. Francis Schaeffer and C. Everett Koop, *Whatever Happened to the Human Race?* (Wheaton, Ill.: Tyndale, 1979).

7. BARRIERS OR BRIDGES?

1. Sidney M. Jourard, *The Transparent Self: Self-Disclosure and Well-Being* (New York: Van Nostrand Reinhold Co., 1971), p. 59. Italics mine.
2. Dietrich Bonhoeffer, *Life Together*, trans. John W. Doberstein (New York: Harper & Row, 1954), pp. 105-6.
3. Jerry D. Hull, "Homosexuality: Some Guidelines for the Church," *One*, 1 (April 1981): 5.

8. QUALIFICATIONS OF A TEAR-CATCHER

1. Henri J. M. Nouwen, *In Memoriam* (Notre Dame, Ind.: Ave Maria Press, 1980), p. 58.

10. THE AGENDA OF A TEAR-CATCHER: CARING, LISTENING, SHARING

1. James Ramey, *Intimate Friendships* (Englewood Clifs, N.J.: Prentice-Hall, 1976), p. 87.
2. Bonhoeffer, *Life Together*, pp. 17-23.
3. Ibid., p. 25.
4. Ibid., p. 30.
5. Ibid., p. 100.
6. Warren Farrell, *The Liberated Man: Freeing Men and Their Relationships with Women* (New York: Random House, 1974), p. 11.
7. Ira J. Tanner, *Healing the Pain of Everyday Loss* (Minneapolis: Winston Press, 1976), p. 29.
8. Bonhoeffer, p. 97.
9. Ibid., p. 98.
10. Rudolph E. Grantham, *Lay Shepherding* (Valley Forge, Pa.: Judson Press, 1980), pp. 64-66.
11. Bill Gaither, "The Family of God" (Nashville: The New Benson Co.).

12. Ben Patterson, "Editorial: What Do You Say?" *The Wittenburg Door* (August-September 1983), p. 34.

11. THE AGENDA OF A TEAR-CATCHER: ENCOURAGING, HELPING, CONFRONTING

1. Paul Tournier, *The Seasons of Life* (Richmond, Va.: John Knox Press, 1961), p. 58.
2. Bonhoeffer, *Life Together*, p. 99, italics mine.
3. W. E. McCumber, "A Conference on Servanthood," *Herald of Holiness* 69 (1 August 1980), p. 18.
4. Tanner, *Healing the Pain of Everyday Loss*, pp. 24-25.
5. Bonhoeffer, p. 106.
6. Tanner, p. 25.
7. R. Lofton Hudson, "Growing With People" in *The Art of Being A Man*, ed. J. Allan Petersen (Wheaton, Ill.: Tyndale, 1973), p. 55.
8. Edwin S. Ufford, "Throw Out the Lifeline" in *Praise and Worship* (Kansas City: Nazarene Publishing House, n.d.), p. 253.
9. *The Upper Room Disciplines* (Nashville: The Upper Room, 1979), p. 134.